3d Edition

Word Division Manual

THE TWENTY THOUSAND MOST-USED WORDS IN BUSINESS COMMUNICATION

DEVERN J. PERRY
Brigham Young University

J.E. SILVERTHORN
Formerly of Oklahoma State University

Published by

K98 **SOUTH-WESTERN PUBLISHING CO.**

CINCINNATI   WEST CHICAGO, ILL.   DALLAS   PELHAM MANOR, N.Y.   PALO ALTO, CALIF.

A B C D E F G H I J K L M N O P Q R S T U V W X Y Z

ISBN: 0-538-11980-2

Library of Congress Catalog Card Number: 83-60229

2 3 4 5 6 7 8 9 H 2 1 0 9 8 7 6 5 4

Printed in the United States of America

Foreword

The Third Edition of WORD DIVISION MANUAL has been revised and updated to meet the increasing and changing needs of its users. This has been accomplished through the inclusion of a large number of additional words and through the incorporation of many excellent suggestions from users.

This edition contains 20,002 words, nearly 5,000 more than the Second Edition. However, this edition deletes many plurals—especially plurals which do not add a syllable to the root word—that appeared in the previous edition. As a result, approximately 7,000 commonly used business words are contained in this edition that did not appear previously. With the ever-increasing vocabulary of the age of technology, this should be a greater help to the user.

Since the publication of the Second Edition, many teachers and other users have taken the time to write the publisher or to share their suggestions with their South-Western marketing representative. All suggestions were carefully reviewed by the author and the editorial staff and, where feasible, were incorporated in this edition.

As with previous editions of WORD DIVISION MANUAL, this edition is based on a word frequency study of the words of business communications. Such a base is necessary to comprehensively incorporate the common words that business users will need for correct spelling and hyphenation. "The Most Frequently Used Words and Phrases of Business Communications" was used as the basis for this edition. This study was prepared by Devern J. Perry with a grant from the Delta Pi Epsilon Research Foundation.

Since this Manual is increasingly used as a spelling reference as well as a word division source, words not appearing in the Perry list were also selected for inclusion. These words were selected from WEBSTER'S NINTH NEW COLLEGIATE DICTIONARY, published by Merriam-Webster Inc. One-syllable words and other words with no preferred division points are included primarily as a spelling reference.

As in previous editions, word division is indicated by both a hyphen and a dot. Preferred word division locations, according to the Guidelines for Word Division, are indicated by a hyphen. Acceptable, but not preferred, points of word division are indicated by a dot. For example, the word "understanding" appears as *un•der-stand•ing* in this Manual. While the word may be correctly divided at any one of three points, the preferred division is indicated by the hyphen. However, a shorter word—such as "effort" *ef•fort*—may be divided at the dot although the preferred choice is to avoid dividing the word.

A double hyphen is used to indicate a compound word. According to the Guidelines for Word Division, these words should be divided only at the hyphen: *self--evaluation*.

For easy reference, these three symbols are listed at the conclusion of this section.

Users of the Second Edition have commented that the compact size of the book makes it very practical and easy to use. This size has been retained in the Third Edition, with the addition of spiral binding to allow the Manual to remain open at the desired page. Additional suggestions and comments to your South-Western marketing representative or editorial staff are always welcome.

Symbols Used in WORD DIVISION MANUAL:

- • point of acceptable, but not preferred, word division: *ex•change*
- - point of preferred word division: *hon-ored*
- -- hyphenated compound word. Word division should occur only at the hyphen: *self--sufficient*

Guidelines for Word Division

Since they are widely accepted, the following guidelines were followed in the preparation of WORD DIVISION MANUAL, Third Edition.

1. Although the most acceptable point at which to divide a word is sometimes a matter of opinion, enough of the word should appear on the first line to give the reader the concept of the entire word, and enough of the word should be carried to the next line to have two significantly sized parts. Word pronunciation is also an important factor in determining the best division point.

2. Words should be divided only between syllables. One-syllable words, such as *called, heights,* and *straight,* must not be divided.

3. In word division, at least two letters must appear with the first part of the word (*in-crease*, but not a-board); and at least three letters must appear with the last part of the word (*start-ing*, but not start-er).

Although acceptable, avoid dividing two letters at the beginning of a word. These *acceptable* but not *preferred* divisions are indicated by a dot rather than a hyphen in this book; for example, *re•li-able.*

4. Regardless of the number of syllables contained in the word, never divide words of five or fewer letters, such as *ideal* and *able.* If possible, avoid dividing words of six letters; for example: *puzzle* is better than *puz-zle.*

5. When adding a suffix to a word produces a double consonant, divide between the two consonants; for example, *slip-pery*, not slipp-ery. However, when the root word ends in a double consonant before the suffix is added, divide between the root word and the suffix; for example, *drill-ing*, not dril-ling.

6. Compounds words which *do not* contain a hyphen should be divided between the elements of the compound, such as *sales-people*, instead of salespeo-ple. Compound words which *do* contain a hyphen should be divided only at the point of the existing hyphen, such as *self--respect.*

7. In general, a single-vowel syllable within a word should be written with the first part of the word, such as *tabu-late,* not tab-ulate.

Exceptions to the general rule:

Join a single-vowel syllable to the last part of the word if the word ends in a two-letter syllable: *real-ity*.

Join single-vowel syllables *a, i,* or *u* to the final syllables *ble, bly, cle,* or *cal*: *favor-able, prefer-ably, mir-acle, med-ical*.

Divide between two one-vowel syllables occurring together within a word: *evalu-ation*.

8. When it is necessary to divide a date, name, or address, divide at the logical point for readability:

Divide between the date and the year (*January 1,-1985*), not between the month and the day (January-1, 1985).

Divide between parts of the name as illustrated: *Mr. Anthony-Fuller*, not Mr.-Anthony Fuller; *Susan-Brown, M.D.*, not Susan Brown, -M.D.

Divide the address between the city and the state (*Cincinnati,-Ohio 45227-1342*), not between the state and the postal zip code (Cincinnati, Ohio-45227-1342).

9. Avoid dividing figures, abbreviations, and signs representing words or abbreviations (*$25,000,* not $25,-000 or $-25,000; *NASA,* not NA-SA; *#462867,* not #-462867; and *15 ft.,* not 15-ft.).

10. The division of words should be minimized. Avoid dividing the last word of more than two consecutive lines. Also avoid dividing the last word of a paragraph or the last word on a page.

11. When determining the points at which to end a line, remember that how the line ends has considerable influence on the degree of ease with which the reader can follow the thought of the written expression. Therefore, the division of words should be logical, with as little attention called to the word division as possible.

A

a
aard-vark
aba•cus
aba-lone
aban-don

aban-doned
aban-don•ing
aban-don-ment
abase
abased

abate
abated
abate-ment
abbey
ab•bre-vi-ate

ab•bre-vi-ated
ab•bre-via-tion
ab•di-cate
ab•di-ca-tion
ab•do-men

ab•domi-nal
ab•duct
ab•duc-tor
ab•er-rant
ab•er-ra-tion

abey-ance
abhor
ab•horred
ab•hor-rence
ab•hor-rent

ab•hor-ring
abide
abid-ing
abili-ties
abil-ity

ab•jure
ablaze
able
ably
ab•nor-mal

ab•nor-mali-ties
ab•nor-mal•ity
ab•nor-mally
aboard
abode

abol-ish
abol-ished
abol-ish•ing
abol-ish-ment
abo-li-tion

abo-li-tion•ist
abomi-na•ble
abomi-na-tion
ab•orig-ine
abort

aborted
abort-ing
abor-tion
abor-tion•ist
abor-tive

abound
about
about--face
above
above--mentioned

abrade
abra-sion
abra-sive
abreast
abridge

abridged
abridg-ment
abroad
ab•ro-gate
ab•ro-gated

abrupt
ab•scess
ab•scessed
ab•scond
ab•sconder

ab•sence
ab•sences
ab•sent
ab•sen-tee
ab•sen-tee•ism

ab•sent-ing
ab•sently
ab•so-lute
ab•so-lutely
ab•so-lu-tion

ab•solve
ab•solved
ab•sorb
ab•sorbed
ab•sor-bency

ab•sor-bent
ab•sorb-ing
ab•sorp-tion
ab•stain
ab•stainer

ab•stract
ab•stracted
ab•stract-ing
ab•strac-tion
ab•strac-tor

ab•surd
abun-dance
abun-dant
abuse
abused

abuses
abus-ing
abu-sive
abut
abut-ment

abut-ter
abut-ting
abyss
aca-de-mia
aca-demic

aca-demi-cal-ly
aca-de-mi-cian
acade-mies
acad-emy
a cap-pella

ac•cede
ac•ceded
ac•ced-ing
ac•cel-er-ate
ac•cel-er-ated

ac•cel-er-at•ing
ac•cel-era-tion
ac•cel-er-ome•ter
ac•cent
ac•cented

ac•cen-tu-ate
ac•cen-tu-ated
ac•cept
ac•cept-abil•ity
ac•cept-able

ac•cept-ably
ac•cep-tance
ac•cep-tances
ac•cepted
ac•cept-ing

ac•cess
ac•ces-si-bil•ity
ac•ces-si•ble
ac•cess-ing
ac•ces-sion

ac•ces-sioned
ac•ces-so-rial
ac•ces-so-ries
ac•ces-sory
ac•ci-dent

ac•ci-den•tal
ac•claim
ac•claimed
ac•cla-ma-tion
ac•cli-mate

ac•cli-ma-tize
ac•co-lade
ac•com-mo-date
ac•com-mo-dated
ac•com-mo-dat•ing

ac•com-mo-da-tion
ac•com-pa-nied
ac•com-pa-nies
ac•com-pa-ni-ment
ac•com-pa-nist

ac•com-pany
ac•com-pa-ny•ing
ac•com-plice
ac•com-plish
ac•com-plished

ac•com-plishes
ac•com-plish•ing
ac•com-plish-ment
ac•cord
ac•cor-dance

ac•corded
ac•cord-ing
ac•cord-ingly
ac•cor-dion
ac•cost

ac•count
ac•count-abil•ity
ac•count-able
ac•coun-tancy
ac•coun-tant

ac•counted
ac•count-ing
ac•credit
ac•credi-ta-tion
ac•cred-ited

ac•cred-it•ing
ac•crual
ac•crue
ac•crued
ac•cru-ing

ac•cu-mu-late
ac•cu-mu-lated
ac•cu-mu-lat•ing
ac•cu-mu-la-tion
ac•cu-mu-la-tive

ac•cu-mu-la-tively
ac•cu-mu-la•tor
ac•cu-ra-cies
ac•cu-racy
ac•cu-rate

ac•cu-rately
ac•cursed
ac•cu-sa-tion
ac•cu-sa-tive
ac•cuse

ac•cused
ac•cus-ing
ac•cus-tom
ac•cus-tomed
ace

ac•er-bate
ace-tate
ace-tone
ace-tyl-sali-cylic
ache

achiev-able
achieved
achieve-ment
achiever
achiev-ers

achiev-ing
ach•ing
acid
acid-ity
aci-dized

ac·knowl-edge
ac·knowl-edged
ac·knowl-edges
ac·knowl-edg·ing
ac·knowl-edg-ment

acne
acous-tic
acous-ti·cal
ac·quaint
ac·quain-tance

ac·quain-tances
ac·quain-tance-ship
ac·quainted
ac·quaint-ing
ac·qui-esce

ac·qui-es-cence
ac·qui-es-cent
ac·quire
ac·quired
ac·quir-ing

ac·qui-si-tion
ac·qui-si-tional
ac·quit
ac·quit-tal
ac·quit-tance

ac·quit-ted
acre
acre-age
acre-ages
Ac·ri-lan

ac·ri-mony
ac·ro-bat
ac·ro-batic
ac·ro-nym
across

acrylic
act
acted
act·ing
ac·tion

ac·ti-vate
ac·ti-vated
ac·ti-vat·ing
ac·ti-va-tion
ac·tive

ac·tively
ac·tiv-ist
ac·tivi-ties
ac·tiv-ity
actor

ac·tress
ac·tual
ac·tu-ally
ac·tu-ar·ial
ac·tu-ar·ies

ac·tu-ary
ac·tu-ate
ac·tu-ated
ac·tua-tor
acu·ity

acu·men
acute
acutely
ad
adage

ada·gio
ada-mant
adapt
adapt-abil·ity
adapt-able

ad·ap-ta-tion
adapted
adapter
adapt-ing
adap-tive

adap-tively
add
added
ad·denda
ad·den-dum

ad·dict
ad·dicted
ad·dic-tion
add·ing
ad·di-tion

ad·di-tional
ad·di-tion-ally
ad·di-tive
ad·dress
ad·dressed

ad·dressee
ad·dresser
ad·dresses
ad·dress-ing
ade-noids

adept
ade-quacy
ade-quate
ade-quately
ad·here

ad·hered
ad·her-ence
ad·her-ent
ad·her-ing
ad·he-sion

ad·he-sive
ad·he-sive-ness
ad hoc
ad in·fi-ni·tum
ad·ja-cent

ad·jec-tive
ad·join
ad·join-ing
ad·journ
ad·journed

ad·journ-ing
ad·journ-ment
ad·judge
ad·judged
ad·ju-di-cate

ad•ju-di-cated
ad•ju-di-ca-tion
ad•ju-di-ca-tory
ad•junct
ad•junc-tive

ad•just
ad•just-able
ad•justed
ad•juster
ad•just-ing

ad•just-ment
ad•justor
ad•ju-tant
ad•min-is•ter
ad•min-is-tered

ad•min-is-ter•ing
ad•min-is-tra-tion
ad•min-is-tra-tive
ad•min-is-tra-tively
ad•min-is-tra•tor

ad•mi-ra•ble
ad•mi-ra•bly
ad•mi-ral
ad•mi-ralty
ad•mi-ra-tion

ad•mire
ad•mired
ad•mis-si-bil•ity
ad•mis-si•ble
ad•mis-sion

admit
ad•mit-tance
ad•mit-ted
ad•mit-tedly
ad•mit-ting

ad•mon-ish
ad•mo-ni-tion
adobe
ado-les-cence
ado-les-cent

adopt
adopted
adopt-ing
adop-tion
adop-tive

ador-able
ado-ra-tion
adorn
adorn-ment
ad•re-nal

adroit
ad•sorb
ad•sor-bent
ad•sorp-tion
ad•sorp-tive

adult
adul-tery
adult-hood
ad va•lo-rem
ad•vance

ad•vanced
ad•vance-ment
ad•vances
ad•vanc-ing
ad•van-tage

ad•van-ta-geous
ad•van-ta-geously
ad•van-tages
ad•vent
ad•ven-ture

ad•ven-tur•ous
ad•verb
ad•ver-bial
ad•ver-sary
ad•verse

ad•versely
ad•ver-sity
ad•ver-tise
ad•ver-tised
ad•ver-tise-ment

ad•ver-tiser
ad•ver-tis•ers
ad•ver-tises
ad•ver-tis•ing
ad•vice

ad•vis-abil•ity
ad•vis-able
ad•vise
ad•vised
ad•visee

ad•vis-ees
ad•vise-ment
ad•viser
ad•vises
ad•vis-ing

ad•vi-sor
ad•vi-sory
ad•vo-cate
ad•vo-cated
ad•vo-cat•ing

aer•ate
aer-at•ing
aera-tion
ae•rial *(adj.)*
ae•ri-al•ist

aero-bal-lis-tics
aero-bic
aero-com-mander
aero-dy-nam•ics
aero-nau-ti•cal

aero-nau-tics
aer-on•omy
aero-sol
aero-space
aes-thetic

aes-theti-cally
aes-thet•ics
af•fa-ble
af•fair
af•fect

af·fec·ta·tion
af·fected
af·fect·ing
af·fec·tion
af·fec·tive

af·fec·tively
af·fi·da·vit
af·fili·ate
af·fili·ated
af·fili·at·ing

af·fili·ation
af·fin·ity
af·firm
af·fir·ma·tion
af·fir·ma·tive

af·fir·ma·tively
af·firmed
af·firm·ing
affix
af·fixed

af·fix·ing
af·flict
af·flicted
af·flic·tion
af·flu·ence

af·flu·ent
af·ford
af·ford·able
af·forded
af·ford·ing

af·for·es·ta·tion
af·front
afield
afloat
afoot

afore·mentioned
afore·said
afraid
aft
after

after·burner
after·glow
after·math
after·noon
after·taste

after·thought
after·wards
again
against
ag·ates

age
aged
age·less
agen·cies
agency

agenda
agen·dum
agent
ages
ag·gra·vate

ag·gra·vated
ag·gra·va·tion
ag·gre·gate
ag·gre·gat·ing
ag·gre·ga·tion

ag·gres·sion
ag·gres·sive
ag·gres·sively
ag·gres·sor
ag·grieved

agile
aging
agi·tate
agi·tated
agi·ta·tion

agi·ta·tor
ag·nos·tic
ago
ago·nize
agony

agree
agree·able
agree·ably
agreed
agree·ing

agree·ment
ag·ri·busi·ness
ag·ri·cul·tural
ag·ri·cul·tur·al·ist
ag·ri·cul·tur·ally

ag·ri·cul·ture
ag·ri·cul·tur·ist
agrono·mist
agron·omy
ahead

aid
aide
aided
aide--de--camp
aid·ing

ail·ing
ail·ment
aim
aimed
aim·ing

aim·less
air
air·borne
air check
air--condition

air--conditioned
air con·di·tioner
air con·di·tion·ing
air·craft
aired

air·frame
air·ing
air·lift
air·line
air·liner

air-mail
air-mailed
air-plane
air-port
air show

air-strip
air•way
air-worthy
air-worthiness
aisle

Ala-bama
a la carte
alac-rity
alarm
alarmed

alarm-ing
alarm-ingly
alarm-ist
Alaska
al•beit

album
al•bums
al•co-hol
al•co-holic
al•co-hol•ism

al•cove
alert
alerted
alert-ing
alert-ness

al•falfa
al•ge-bra
al•go-rithm
al•go-rith•mic
alias

alibi
alien
alien-abil•ity
alien-ate
alien-at•ing

alien-ation
align
aligned
align-ment
alike

ali-mony
ali-phatic
alive
al•kali
al•ka-line

all
al•le-ga-tion
al•lege
al•leged
al•leg-edly

al•leges
al•le-giance
al•leg-ing
al•le-gory
al•ler-gic

al•ler-gies
al•lergy
al•le-vi•ate
al•le-vi-ated
al•le-vi-at•ing

alley
al•li-ance
al•lied
al•li-ga•tor
al•lo-cate

al•lo-cated
al•lo-cat•ing
al•lo-ca-tion
allot
al•lot-ment

al•lot-ted
allow
al•low-able
al•low-ance
al•low-ances

al•lowed
al•low-ing
al•lows
alloy
al•loys

al•lude
al•luded
al•lud-ing
al•lure
al•lur-ing

al•lu-sion
al•lu-vium
al•ma-nac
al•mond
al•most

alone
along
along-side
aloud
alpha

al•pha-bet
al•pha-betic
al•pha-bet-ical
al•pha-beti-cally
al•pha-bet•ize

al•pha-nu-meric
al•pine
al•ready
also
altar

alter
al•ter-abil•ity
al•ter-ation
al•ter-cate
al•ter-ca-tion

al•tered
al•ter-ing
al•ter-nate
al•ter-nated
al•ter-nately

al•ter-nat•ing
al•ter-na-tion
al•ter-na-tive
al•ter-na•tor
al•though

al•time-ter
al•ti-tude
al•ti-tu-di•nal
al•to-gether
al•tru-ism

al•tru-is•tic
alu-mi-nous
alu-mi-num
alum-nae
alumni

alum-nus
al•ways
am
amal-gam-ation
amass

ama-teur
ama-teur•ish
amaze
amazed
amaze-ment

amaz-ing
amaz-ingly
am•bas-sa•dor
amber
am•bi-dex•ter•ity

am•bi-dex-trous
am•bi-ence
am•bi-ent
am•bi-gu•ity
am•bigu-ous

am•bi-tion
am•bi-tious
am•biva-lence
am•biva-lent
am•bu-lance

am•bu-lances
am•bu-la-tory
am•bush
ame-lio-rate
ame-lio-ra-tion

ame-na-bil•ity
ame-na•ble
amend
amend-able
amen-da-tory

amended
amend-ing
amend-ment
ame-ni-ties
ame-nity

Amer-ica
Ameri-can
amia-bil•ity
ami-able
ami-ca-bil•ity

ami-ca•ble
amid
am•ines
amino
amity

am•mo-nia
am•mu-ni-tion
am•ne-sia
am•nesty
among

amongst
amoral
amo-rous
am•or-ti-za-tion
am•or-tize

am•or-tized
am•or-tiz•ing
amount
amounted
amount-ing

amp
am•pere
am•per-sand
am•phib-ian
am•phi-the•ater

ample
am•pli-fi-ca-tion
am•pli-fied
am•pli-fier
am•plify

amply
am•pu-tate
am•pu-tated
am•pu-ta-tion
am•pu-tee

amuse
amused
amuse-ment
amus-ing
an

an•aes-the•sia
an•aes-thetic
ana-gram
an•al-ge•sia
an•al-ge•sic

ana•log
analo-gous
anal-ogy
analy-ses
analy-sis

ana-lyst
ana-lytic
ana-lyt-ical
ana-lyze
ana-lyzed

ana-lyzes
ana-lyz•ing
an•ar-chism
an•ar-chist
an•ar-chy

anat-omy
an•ces-tor
an•ces-tral
an•ces-try
an•chor

an•chored
an•cient
an•ciently
an•cil-lary
and

an•ec-dotal
an•ec-dote
ane•mia
ane•mic
an•es-the•sia

an•es-the-si-olo-gist
an•es-thetic
anes-the-tist
anes-the-tize
angel

an•gelic
an•gels
angle
an•gles
an•gling

angry
an•guish
an•guished
an•gu-lar
ani•mal

ani-mate
ani-mated
ani-ma-tion
ani-mos•ity
ankle

annal
an•nals
an•neal
an•nealed
an•neal-ing

annex
an•nex-ation
an•nexed
an•nexes
an•ni-hi-late

an•ni-hi-la-tion
an•ni-ver-sa-ries
an•ni-ver-sary
an•no-tate
an•no-tated

an•no-ta-tion
an•nounce
an•nounced
an•nounce-ment
an•nouncer

an•nounc-ers
an•nounces
an•nounc-ing
annoy
an•noy-ance

an•noyed
an•noy-ing
an•nual
an•nual-ize
an•nual-ized

an•nu-ally
an•nu-ities
an•nu-ity
annul
an•nu-lar

an•nul-ment
an•nu-lus
anode
an•od-ize
anoint

anoma-lies
anoma-lous
anom-aly
ano-nym•ity
anony-mous

an•other
an•oxia
an•oxic
an•swer
an•swer-able

an•swered
an•swer-ing
ant-acid
an•tago-nism
an•tago-nist

an•tago-nis•tic
an•tago-nize
ant-arc•tic
ant-eater
an•te-ced•ent

an•te-date
an•te-di-lu-vian
an•te-lope
an•te-na•tal
an•tenna

an•te-rior
an•te-ri-orly
an•them
an•thol-ogy
an•thro-pol•ogy

an•ti-bi-otic
an•ti-body
an•tici-pate
an•tici-pated
an•tici-pat•ing

an•tici-pa-tion
an•ti-cli•max
an•ti-dis•crimi-na-tion
an•ti-di•ver-sion
an•ti-dote

an•ti-freeze
an•ti-graf-fiti
an•ti-grav•ity
an•ti-his-ta-mine
an•ti-knock

an·ti-mag-netic
an·ti-mis-sile
an·ti-pov-erty
an·ti-quate
an·ti-quated

an·tique
an·tiq-uity
an·ti-so·cial
an·ti-stigma
an·tithe-sis

an·ti-toxic
an·ti-trust
ant·ler
ant-onym
anxi-eties

anxi-ety
anx-ious
anx-iously
any
any-body

any·how
any-more
any·one
any-place
any-thing

any-time
any·way
any·where
apart
apart-ment

apa-thetic
apa·thy
aphid
api·ary
apoca-lypse

apoca-lyp·tic
apo·gee
apolo·getic
apolo-gies
apolo-gize

apolo-gized
apolo-giz·ing
apol-ogy
apos-tasy
apos-tate

apos-ta-tize
apos-tille
apos-tle
apos-to-late
apos-tro·phe

ap·pall
ap·palled
ap·pa-ra·tus
ap·parel
ap·par-ent

ap·par-ently
ap·pa-ri-tion
ap·peal
ap·pealed
ap·peal-ing

ap·pear
ap·pear-ance
ap·pear-ances
ap·peared
ap·pear-ing

ap·pease
ap·peases
ap·pel-lant
ap·pel-late
ap·pend

ap·pend-age
ap·pen-dec-tomy
ap·pended
ap·pen-di-ci·tis
ap·pen-dix

ap·per-tain
ap·pe-tite
ap·pe-tizer
ap·plaud
ap·plauded

ap·plaud-ing
ap·plause
apple
ap·ples
ap·pli-ance

ap·pli-ances
ap·pli-ca-bil·ity
ap·pli-ca·ble
ap·pli-cant
ap·pli-ca-tion

ap·pli-ca·tor
ap·plied
ap·plies
apply
ap·ply-ing

ap·point
ap·pointed
ap·poin-tee
ap·point-ing
ap·point-ment

ap·por-tion
ap·por-tioned
ap·por-tion·ing
ap·por-tion-ment
ap·po-si-tion

ap·posi-tive
ap·praisal
ap·praise
ap·praised
ap·praiser

ap·prais-ing
ap·pre-cia·ble
ap·pre-cia·bly
ap·pre-ci·ate
ap·pre-ci-ated

ap·pre-ci-at·ing
ap·pre-cia-tion
ap·pre-cia-tive
ap·pre-cia-tively
ap·pre-hend

ap·pre-hen-sion
ap·pre-hen-sive
ap·pren-tice
ap·pren-tices
ap·pren-tice-ship

ap·prise
ap·prised
ap·pris-ing
ap·proach
ap·proach-able

ap·proached
ap·proaches
ap·proach-ing
ap·pro-pri·ate
ap·pro-pri-ated

ap·pro-pri-ately
ap·pro-pri-ate-ness
ap·pro-pri-at·ing
ap·pro-pria-tion
ap·prov-able

ap·proval
ap·prove
ap·proved
ap·prov-ing
ap·proxi-mate

ap·proxi-mated
ap·proxi-mately
ap·proxi-mat·ing
ap·proxi-ma-tion
apri-cot

April
apron
aprons
ap·ro-pos
ap·ti-tude

aqua-ma·rine
aquar-ium
aquatic
aq·ue-duct
ar·able

ar·bi-tra·ble
ar·bi-trarily
ar·bi-trary
ar·bi-trate
ar·bi-tra-tion

ar·bi-tra-tor
arbor
arc
ar·cade
arch

ar·chaeo-log-ical
ar·chae-olo-gist
ar·chaic
arched
arch-enemy

ar·chery
arches
ar·chi-tect
ar·chi-tec-tural
ar·chi-tec-tur-ally

ar·chi-tec-ture
ar·chi-val
ar·chive
ar·chi-vist
arc·tic

ar·du-ous
are
area
area-wide
arena

are·nas
aren't
ar·gu-able
argue
ar·gued

ar·gues
ar·gu-ing
ar·gu-ment
ar·gu-men-ta-tive
ar·gyle

arise
arisen
arises
aris-ing
aris-to-crat

arith-me·tic
Ari-zona
Ar·kan-sas
arm
ar·ma-ment

ar·ma-ture
arm-chair
armed
armies
armor

ar·mored
ar·mory
army
aroma
aro-matic

arose
around
arouse
aroused
arouses

ar·raign
ar·raigned
ar·raign-ment
ar·range
ar·ranged

ar·range-ment
ar·ranges
ar·rang-ing
array
ar·rear-age

ar·rears
ar·rest
ar·rested
ar·rest-ing
ar·rival

ar•rive
ar•rived
ar•riv-ing
ar•ro-gance
ar•ro-gant

arrow
arrow-head
ar•rows
ar•se-nal
ar•se-nic

arson
ar•son-ist
art
ar•te-rial
ar•ter-ies

ar•te-rio-scle-ro•sis
ar•tery
ar•thritic
ar•thri-tis
ar•ti-choke

ar•ti-cle
ar•ticu-late
ar•ticu-lated
ar•ticu-lat•ing
ar•ticu-la-tion

ar•ti-facts
ar•ti-fi-cial
ar•ti-fi-cially
ar•til-lery
art•ist

ar•tis-tic
ar•tis-ti-cally
art-istry
art-work
as

as•bes-tos
as•cend
as•cen-dancy
as•cend-ing
as•cent

as•cer-tain
as•cer-tained
as•cer-tain•ing
as•cribe
ash

ashamed
ashes
ashore
aside
asi-nine

ask
asked
ask•ing
as•para-gus
as•pect

aspen
as•phalt
as•pi-rant
as•pi-rate
as•pi-rat•ing

as•pi-ra-tion
as•pire
as•pi-rin
as•pir-ing
as•sail-ant

as•sas-sin
as•sas-si-nate
as•sault
assay
as•sem-blage

as•sem-ble
as•sem-bled
as•sem-bler
as•sem-blies
as•sem-bling

as•sem-bly
as•sented
as•sert
as•serted
as•ser-tion

as•ser-tive
as•sess
as•sess-able
as•sessed
as•sesses

as•sess-ing
as•sess-ment
as•ses-sor
asset
as•sets

as•sign
as•sign-able
as•signed
as•signee
as•sign-ing

as•sign-ment
as•signor
as•simi-late
as•simi-lated
as•simi-lat•ing

as•simi-la-tion
as•sist
as•sis-tance
as•sis-tant
as•sis-tant-ship

as•sisted
as•sist-ing
as•so-ci•ate
as•so-ci-ated
as•so-ci-at•ing

as•so-cia-tion
as•sort
as•sorted
as•sort-ment
as•sume

as•sumed
as•sum-ing
as•sump-tion
as•sur-ance
as•sur-ances

as•sure
as•sured
as•sur-ing
as•ter-isk
as•ter-oid

asthma
asth-matic
astig-ma-tism
as•ton-ish
as•ton-ish•ing

as•ton-ish-ment
as•tound
as•tound-ing
astray
as•trin-gent

as•trol-ogy
as•tro-naut
as•tro-nom-ical
as•tron-omy
as•tute

as•tute-ness
asy•lum
at
athe-ism
ath-lete

ath-letic
ath-leti-cally
atlas
at•mo-sphere
at•mo-spheric

atomic
atroc-ity
at•tach
at•ta-ché
at•tached

at•taches
at•tach-ing
at•tach-ment
at•tack
at•tacked

at•tack-ing
at•tain
at•tain-able
at•tained
at•tain-ing

at•tain-ment
at•tempt
at•tempted
at•tempt-ing
at•tend

at•ten-dance
at•ten-dant
at•tended
at•tend-ees
at•tend-ing

at•ten-tion
at•ten-tive
at•tenu-ate
at•tenu-at•ing
at•tenu-ation

at•test
at•tested
at•test-ing
attic
at•tire

at•ti-tude
at•ti-tu-di•nal
at•tor-ney
at•tract
at•tracted

at•tract-ing
at•trac-tion
at•trac-tive
at•trac-tively
at•trac-tive-ness

at•trib-ut-able
at•tri-bute *(n.)*
at•trib-ute *(v.)*
at•trib-uted
at•tri-tion

atyp-ical
auc-tion
auc-tion•eer
au•dac-ity
au•di-ble

au•di-bly
au•di-ence
au•di-ences
audio
au•dio-logic

au•dio-log-ical
au•di-ol•ogy
audio-visual
audit
au•dited

au•ditee
au•dit-ing
au•di-tion
au•di-tor
au•di-to-rium

au•di-tory
au•dits
auger
aug-ment
aug-mented

Au•gust
aunt
aura
aus-pices
aus-pi-cious

aus-ter•ity
au•then-tic
au•then-ti-cate
au•then-ti-cated
au•then-ti-cat•ing

au•then-ti-ca-tion
au•then-tic•ity
au•thor
au•thored
au•thori-ta-tive

au·thori-ta-tively
au·thori-ties
au·thor-ity
au·tho-ri-za-tion
au·tho-rize

au·tho-rized
au·tho-rizes
au·tho-riz·ing
au·tis-tic
au·tis-ti-cally

auto
au·to-bio-graph-ical
au·to-bi-og-ra·phy
au·to-clave
au·to-graph

au·to-mate
au·to-mated
au·to-matic
au·to-mati-cally
au·to-mat·ing

au·to-ma-tion
au·toma-tize
au·to-mo-bile
au·to-mo-tive
au·tono-mous

au·ton-omy
au·to-pi·lot
au·top-sies
au·topsy
au·tumn

aux-il-ia-ries
aux-il-iary
avail
avail-abil·ity
avail-able

avail-ing
ava-lanche
avenge
ave·nue
aver

av·er-age
av·er-aged
av·er-ages
av·er-ag·ing
averse

aver-sion
avert
averted
avia-tion
avia-tor

av·idly
avi-on·ics
avo-ca-tion
avoid
avoid-ance

avoided
avoid-ing
await
awaited
await-ing

awake
awak-ened
awak-en·ing
award
awarded

award-ing
aware
aware-ness
away
awe-some

awful
aw·fully
awhile
awk-ward
aw·ning

awoke
awry
axial
axi-om-atic
axis

axle

B

_ **B** _____

bab·ble
ba·bies
baby
ba·by-ish
bac-ca-lau-re·ate

bache-lor
back
back-ache
back-bone
back-drop

backed
back-fire
back-ground
back-haul
back-hoe

back-ing
back-lash
back-log
back-packing
back-side

backup
back-wards
bac-te·ria
bac-te-rial
bac-te-ri-cide

bac-te-ri-ol·ogy
bad
badge
badges
badly

bad-min·ton
baf·fle
bag
bag-gage
bagged

bag-ging
bag-pipe
bail
bai-liff
bai-li-wick

bait
bake
baked
baker
bak•ers

bak•ery
bak•ing
bal-ance
bal-anced
bal-ances

bal-anc•ing
bal-co-nies
bal-cony
bald
balk

balked
ball
bal•lad
bal-last
bal•let

ball field
bal-lis•tic
bal-loon
bal-lot
bal-lot•ing

ball-room
ba•lo-ney
bal•sam
bam•boo
ba•nana

band
ban-dage
ban-danna
banded
band-ing

ban•dit
band-wagon
bang
banged
bang-ing

ban•ish
ban-ishes
ban-ish-ment
banjo
bank

bank-card
banked
banker
bank-ers
bank-ing

bank-rupt
bank-rupt-cies
bank-ruptcy
banned
ban•ner

ban-quet
bap-tism
bap-tize
bar
bar-bar•ian

bar-baric
bar-be•cue
bar•ber
bare
barely

bar-gain
bar-gained
bar-gain•ing
barge
barges

bari-tone
bark
barker
bar•ley
barn

ba•rome-ter
ba•roque
bar-rage
barred
bar•rel

bar-rels
bar•ren
bar-ri-cade
bar-ri-caded
bar-rier

bar-ring
bar-ris•ter
bar-tender
bar•ter
basal

base
base-ball
based
base-line
base-ment

bases
bash-ful
basic
ba•si-cally
ba•sics

basin
bas•ing
basis
bas•ket
basket-ball

bas•set
bas-si•net
bat
batch
batches

bate
bated
bath
bathe
bath-house

bath-ing
bath-robe
bath-room
bath-tub
baton

bat-tal-ion
bat-ted
bat-ter
bat-tered
bat-ter-ies

bat-tery
bat-ting
bat-tle
bat-tled
battle-field

battle-ground
bat-tle-ment
battle-ship
bay
bayo-net

ba-zaar
be
beach
beaches
bea-con

bea-dle
beam
beam-ing
bean
bear

bear-able
beard
bearer
bear-ing
beast

beat
beaten
beat-ing
beau-ti-cian
beau-ti-fi-ca-tion

beau-ti-ful
beau-ti-fully
beau-tify
beau-ti-fy-ing
beauty

bea-ver
be-came
be-cause
beckon
be-come

be-com-ing
bed
bed-ded
bed-ding
bed-fast

bed-lam
bed-pan
bed-rid-den
bed-rock
bed-room

bed-side
bed-sores
bed-spread
beef
bee-hive

bee-keeper
been
beer
bees-wax
bee-tles

be-fall
be-fit-ting
be-fore
be-fore-hand
be-friend

began
beg-gar
begin
be-gin-ner
be-gin-ning

be-grudge
be-guile
begun
be-half
be-have

be-hav-ing
be-hav-ior
be-hav-ioral
be-hind
be-hold

be-hoove
beige
being
be-la-bor
be-lated

be-lat-edly
be-lief
be-lieve
be-lieved
be-liever

be-liev-ing
be-lit-tle
bell
bel-lig-er-ence
bel-lig-er-ent

belly-ache
be-long
be-longed
be-long-ing
be-loved

below
belt
belted
belt-ing
belt-way

bench
benches
bend
bend-ing
be-neath

bene-dic-tion
bene-fac-tor
bene-fi-cial
bene-fi-cia-ries
bene-fi-ciary

bene-fit
bene-fited
bene-fit·ing
be·nevo-lence
be·nevo-lent

be·nign
bent
ben-zene
be·queath
be·queathed

be·quest
be·reave
be·reave-ment
ber-serk
berth

be·seech
be·side
be·siege
be·sieged
be·speak

best
be·stow
be·stowed
bet
be·tray

be·trayed
be·tray-ing
be·troth
be·trothal
be·trothed

bet·ter
bet·ter-ment
bet-ting
be·tween
bevel

bev-eled
bev-er·age
bev-er-ages
be·ware
be·wil-der

be·wil-dered
be·wil-dering
be·yond
bi·an-nual
bi·an-nu-ally

bias
bi·ased
bible
bi·bles
bib-li·cal

bib·li-og-ra·pher
bib·lio-graphic
bib·lio-graph-ical
bib·li-og-ra·phies
bib·li-og-ra·phy

bi·car-bon·ate
bi·cen-ten-nial
bi·ceps
bicker
bick-er·ing

bi·cy-cle
bi·cy-clist
bid
bid·der
bid-ding

bi·en-nial
bi·en-ni-ally
bi·fo-cals
big
big·ger

big-gest
big-otry
bike
bi·kini
bi·lat-eral

bi·lat-er-ally
bi·lin-ear
bi·lin-gual
bill
bill-board

billed
bil·let
bill-fold
bil-liards
bill-ing

bil-lion
bi·monthly
bi·nary
bi·na-tional
bind

binder
bind-ers
bind-ery
bind-ing
bin-ocu·lar

bio-chem-ical
bio-chem-is·try
bio-de·grad-able
bio·feed-back
bi·og-ra-pher

bio-graphic
bio-graph-ical
bi·og-ra·phy
bio-log-ical
bi·ol-ogy

bio-med-ical
bi·opsy
bio·syn-thetic
bi·otic
bi·par-ti·san

bi·plane
bird
birth
birth-day
bis-cuit

bi·sect
bishop
bit
bite
bit·ing

bit·ter
bit·ter·est
bit·terly
bit·ter·ness
bitter-sweet

bi·tu·mi·nous
bi·weekly
bi·zarre
black
blacken

black-en·ing
black-mail
black-out
black-smith
black-top

blad-der
blade
blame
blame-less
blam-ing

blank
blan-ket
blas-phe-mous
blas-phemy
blast

blasted
blaster
blast-ing
bla-tant
blazer

blaz-ing
bleacher
bleach-ing
bleak
bled

bleed
bleed-ing
blem-ish
blem-ishes
blend

blended
blender
blend-ing
bless
blessed

bless-ing
blew
blind
blind-fold
blind-ing

blind-ness
blink
blinker
bliss
bliss-ful

blis-ter
blitz
bliz-zard
block
block-ade

block-age
block-buster
blocked
blocker
block-ing

blond
blond-ish
blood
bloom
bloom-ing

blos-som
blot
blot-ter
blot-ting
blouse

blow
blower
blow-ers
blow-ing
blown

blow-out
blow·up
blud-geon
blue
blue-berry

blue--green
blue-print
bluff
blu·ish
blun-der

blunt
bluntly
blur
blurred
blurry

board
boarded
boarder
board-ing
board-walk

boast
boast-ful
boat
boater
boat-ing

boat-swain
bob·bin
bob·ble
bod·ied
bod·ies

bodily
body
body-guard
bogged
bogus

boil
boiled
boiler
boil-ers
bois-ter•ous

bold
bold-face
bo•lo-gna
bol-ster
bolt

bolted
bomb
bom-bard
bom-bard•ing
bom-bard-ment

bomber
bomb-ing
bomb-proof
bona fide
bo•nanza

bond
bond-age
bonded
bond-holder
bond-ing

bone
bon-fire
bonnet-ball
bonus
bo•nuses

book
book-binder
book-case
book-cases
book-dealer

book-dealers
booked
booker
book-ing
book-ish

book-keeper
book-keepers
book-keeping
book-let
book-maker

book-mark
book-seller
book-store
boom
boo-mer•ang

boom-ing
boon
boost
boosted
booster

boost-ing
boot
booth
boot-leg
boot-strap

bor•der
bor-dered
bor-der•ing
border-line
bore

bore-dom
bor•ing
born
borne
bor•row

bor-rowed
bor-rower
bor-row•ers
bor-row•ing
boss

bosses
bo•tan-ical
bota-nist
bot•any
both

bother
both-ered
both-er•ing
both•er-some
bot•tle

bottle-neck
bot-tler
bot-tling
bot•tom
bot-tomed

bot-tom•ing
bot•tom-less
botu-lism
bought
bouil-lon

boul-der
bou-le-vard
bounce
bounc-ing
bound

bound-aries
bound-ary
bounded
bound-ing
bound-less

boun-te•ous
boun-ti•ful
bounty
bou-quet
bour-bon

bou-tique
bou-ton-niere
bow
bow•els
bow•ery

bowl
bowler
bowl-ing
box
boxed

boxer
boxes
box·ing
boy
boy-cott

boy-cotted
brace
brace-let
brac-ing
bracket

brack-eted
brack-ish
brag
brag-gart
bragged

brag-ging
braid
braille
brain
brain-less

brain-storm
brain-storming
brain-wash
brain-washing
braised

brake
branch
branches
branch-ing
brand

branded
brand-ing
brass
bras-siere
brave

brav-ery
bra·zen
braz-ing
breach
breaches

bread
breadth
bread-winner
break
break-age

break-away
break-down
breaker
break-ers
break-fast

break--in *(n.)*
break-ing
break-out *(n.)*
breast
breath

breathe
breather
breath-ing
breath-less
breath-taking

bred
breed
breeder
breed-ers
breed-ing

breeze
breezy
brev-ity
brewer
brew-er·ies

brew-ery
brew-ing
bribe
brib-ery
brick

brick-bat
brick-layer
bridal
bride-groom
bridge

bridges
bridg-ing
bri·dle
brief
brief-case

briefed
brief-est
brief-ing
briefly
bri-gade

briga-dier
bright
brighten
brighter
bright-est

brightly
bright-ness
bril-liance
bril-liant
bril-liantly

bring
bring-ing
brink
bri-quette
bris-tle

brit-tle
broach
broached
broad
broad-cast

broad-casted
broad-caster
broad-cast·ing
broaden
broad-ened

broad-en·ing
broader
broad-est
broad-loom
broadly

broad--minded
broad-side
Broad-way
bro-cade
broc-coli

bro-chure
brogue
broil
broiled
broiler

broke
bro•ken
bro•ker
bro•ker-age
bro•kered

bron-chial
bron-chitic
bron-chi•tis
bronco
bronze

brooch
brood
brood-ing
brook
broom

broom-stick
brother
broth-ers
brought
brown

browned
brown-ish
browse
bruises
bruis-ing

brushed
brush-ing
brusque
bru-tal•ity
bru-tally

bub•ble
bub-bled
buc-ca-neer
buck
bucka-roo

bucket
buck•et-ful
buckle
buck-led
buck-ling

bud-dies
bud-ding
buddy
bud•get
bud-get•ary

bud-geted
bud-get•ing
buff
buf-falo
buffed

buffer
buff-ered
buff-ers
buf•fet
buff-ing

bugle
build
builder
build-ers
build-ing

buildup
built
built--in
bulb
bul-bous

bulge
bulg-ing
bulk
bulk-head
bulky

bull
bull-dozer
bull-doz•ing
bul•let
bul-le•tin

bull-headed
bull-ish
bull-ock
bul-wark
bumble-bee

bump
bumped
bumper
bump-ers
bump-ing

bunch
bun•dle
bun-dled
bun-ga•low
bun•gle

bunk beds
bun•ker
bun-ting
buoy
buoy-ancy

buoy-ant
bur•den
bur-dened
bur•den-some
bu•reau

bu•reau-cracy
bu•reau-crat
bu•reau-cratic
bur-geon
bur-geoned

bur-geon•ing
bur-glar
bur-glar•ies
bur-glar•ize
burglar-proof

bur-glary
burial
bur•ied
bur•lap
bur-lesque

burn
burned
burner
burn-ing
burn-out

burnt
bur•row
bur•sar
bur-si•tis
burst

burst-ing
bus
bush
bushel
bushes

busier
busi-est
busily
busi-ness
busi-nesses

business-man
business-woman
bus•ses
bus-sing
busy

but
bu•tane
but•ler
but•ter
but-tered

butter-fly
butter-milk
but-tery
but•ton
but-toned

button-hole
but-ton•ing
buy
buyer
buy•ers

buy•ing
by
bylaw
by•laws
by--line

by•pass
by•pass-ing
by--product
by•stander

C

cab
caba-ret
cab-bage
cabin
cabi-net

cable
ca•ble-gram
ca•bles
ca•boose
ca•chet

cac•tus
ca•daver
cad•die
ca•dence
cadet

café
cafe-te•ria
cafe-to-rium
caf-feine
cage

ca•hoots
ca•jole
cake
cake-walk
ca•lami-tous

ca•lam-ity
cal-cium
cal-cu-late
cal-cu-lated
cal-cu-lat•ing

cal-cu-la-tion
cal-cu-la•tor
cal-culi
cal-cu•lus
cal-en•dar

cal-en-dars
calf
cali-ber
cali-brate
cali-brated

cali-bra-tion
calico
Cali-for•nia
cali-pers
cal-is-then•ics

call
call-back
called
caller
call-ers

call-ing
cal-li•ope
cal-lous
calm
calmly

calo-ries
cal•orie
calves
cam
ca•ma-ra-de•rie

C

cam-bric
came
ca•mel-lia
cam•era
cam-ou-flage

camp
cam-paign
cam-paigned
cam-paigner
cam-paign•ing

camper
camp-ing
camp-site
cam•pus
cam-puses

can
Can•ada
canal
ca•nals
ca•nary

can•cel
can-cel-la-tion
can-celed
can-cel•ing
can•cer

can•did
can-di-dacy
can-di-date
can-didly
can-died

can-dies
can•dle
can•dor
candy
ca•nine

can-is•ter
canned
can-nery
can-ni•bal
can-ning

can•non
can•not
canoe
ca•noes
can•opy

can't
can-ta-loupe
can-teen
can•ton
can•vas

can-vass
can-vassed
can-vasser
can-vass•ing
can•yon

ca•pa-bili-ties
ca•pa-bil•ity
ca•pa-ble
ca•pa-bly
ca•paci-ties

ca•paci-tor
ca•pac-ity
cape
cap-il-lary
capi-tal

capi-tal•ism
capi-tal•ist
capi-tal-is•tic
capi-tal-iza-tion
capi-tal•ize

capi-tal-ized
capi-tol
capped
ca•pri-cious
cap-size

cap-sule
cap-tain
cap-tion
cap-tioned
cap-tion•ing

cap-ti-vate
cap-tive
cap-tiv•ity
cap•tor
cap-ture

cap-tured
cap-tur•ing
car
cara-mel
carat

cara-van
car-bide
car•bon
car-bon•ate
car-bon-ized

car-bon-iz•ing
car-bu-re•tor
car-cass
car-casses
car-ci-no-ge-nic•ity

card
card-board
card-holder
car-diac
car-di•gan

car-di•nal
car-di-olo-gist
car-dio-re•spi-ra-tory
car-dio-vas•cu•lar
care

cared
ca•reer
care-free
care-ful
care-fully

care-less
care-lessly
care-less-ness
ca•ress
care-taker

cargo
car-goes
cari-ca-ture
car•ing
car-load

car-na-tion
car-ni•val
carol
car-ou•sel
car-pen•ter

car-pen•try
car•pet
car-peted
car-pet•ing
car-pool

car-pooler
car-pooling
car-port
car•rel
car-riage

car-ried
car-rier
car-ri•ers
car-ries
car•rot

carry
car-ry•ing
carry--over
cart
cart-age

car•tel
car-ti-lage
car-to-graph-ical
car-tog-ra•phy
car•ton

car-toon
car-tridge
car-tridges
cas-cade
case

case-book
cased
case-load
case-ment
cases

case-work
case-worker
cash
cashed
cashes

cash-ier
cash-ing
cash-mere
cas•ing
ca•sino

cas•ket
cas-se-role
cas-sette
cast
caste

caster
cas-ti-gate
cast-ing
cas•tle
cast--off *(adj.)*

ca•sual
ca•su-ally
ca•su-al-ties
ca•su-alty
cata-log

cata-loged
cata-log•ing
cata-lyst
cata-lytic
cata-ract

ca•tas-tro•phe
cata-strophic
catch
catch-all
catcher

catches
catch-ing
cate-gor-ical
cate-gori-cally
cate-go-ries

cate-go-rize
cate-go-rized
cate-go-riz•ing
cate-gory
cater

ca•tered
ca•terer
ca•ter-ing
cat•er-pil•lar
cat-fish

ca•the-dral
cathe-ter
cath-ode
cat•sup
cat•tle

Cau-ca-sian
cau•cus
caught
cau-li-flower
caulk

caulk-ing
cause
caused
causes
caus-ing

caus-tic
cau-tion
cau-tioned
cau-tious
cau-tiously

cav-alry
cav•ern
cav•iar
cavi-ties
cav•ity

cease	cen-tral	chalk-board
ceased	cen-tral-iza-tion	chal-lenge
cease--fire	cen-tral•ize	chal-lenged
ceases	cen-tral-ized	chal-lenges
cedar	cen-tral-izes	chal-leng•ing
cede	cen-tral-iz•ing	cham-ber
ceded	cen-trally	cham-bray
ced•ing	cen-trifu•gal	cham-fer
ceil-ing	cen-trifu-gally	cham-ois
cele-brate	cen-tri-fuge	cham-pagne
cele-brated	cen-tu-ries	cham-pion
cele-brat•ing	cen-tury	cham-pion-ship
cele-bra-tion	ce•ram-ics	chance
ce•leb-ri•ties	ce•real	chan-cel•lor
ce•leb-rity	ce•re-bral	chan-cery
cel•ery	cere-mo-nial	chances
celi-bacy	cere-mo-ni-ally	chan-de-lier
cell	cere-mo-nies	change
cel•lar	cere-mony	change-able
cel-lo-phane	cer-tain	changed
cel-lu-loid	cer-tainly	change-over
cel-lu-lose	cer-tainty	changes
ce•ment	cer-tifi-cate	chang-ing
ce•mented	cer-tifi-cated	chan-nel
ceme-tery	cer-ti-fi-ca-tion	chan-neled
ce•ment-ing	cer-ti-fied	chaos
cen•sor	cer-ti-fies	cha-otic
cen-sored	cer-tify	cha•pel
cen-sor-ship	cer-ti-fy•ing	cha-pels
cen-sure	cer-vi•cal	chap-eron
cen•sus	ces-sa-tion	chap-lain
cent	cha-grin	chap-ter
cen-ten-nial	chain	char-ac•ter
cen•ter	chair	char-ac-ter-is•tic
cen-tered	chaired	char-ac-ter-is-ti-cally
cen-ter•ing	chair-man	char-ac-ter-iza-tion
center-piece	chair-person	char-ac-ter•ize
center-pieces	chair-woman	char-ac-ter-ized
cen-ti-grade	cha•let	cha-rade
cen-ti-me•ter	chalk	char-coal

charge
charge-abil·ity
charge-able
charge--back
charged

charger
charges
charg-ing
char-iot
cha-risma

chari-ta·ble
chari-ties
char-ity
char-la·tan
charm

charmed
charm-ing
chart
charted
char-ter

char-tered
char-ter·ing
chart-ing
chase
chases

chas-ing
chas-sis
chas-tise
chas-tise-ment
chas-tity

châ-teau
chat-tel
chat-ter
chauf-feur
chau-vin·ism

chau-vin·ist
cheap
cheapen
cheaper
cheap-est

cheaply
cheat
cheat-ing
check
check-book

checked
checker
checker-board
check-ered
check-ers

check-ing
check-list
check-mate
check-out
checkup

cheer
cheered
cheer-ful
cheer-fully
cheer-ing

cheer-leader
cheese
chem-ical
chemi-cally
chem-ist

chem-is·try
che-mo-ther·apy
che-nille
cher-ish
cher-ished

cher-ries
cherry
chest
chest-nut
chew

chew-ing
chicken
chick-ens
chide
chided

chief
chiefly
chif-fon
child
child-bearing

child-birth
child-hood
child-ish
child-less
chil-dren

chili
chill
chilled
chilly
chim-ney

chim-pan·zee
china
china-ware
Chi-nook
chip

chipped
chip-per
chip-ping
chi-ro-prac·tic
chi-ro-prac·tor

chisel
chis-eled
chis-el·ing
chiv-alry
chlo-ride

chlo-ri-nate
chlo-ri-nated
chlo-ri-na-tion
chlo-rine
chlo-ro-form

chlo-ro-phyll
choco-late
choice
choices
choir

choir-master
choke
choked
chok-ing
cho-les-terol

choose
chooses
choos-ing
chop
chopped

chop-per
choppy
chop-sticks
cho-ral
cho-reo-graph

cho-re-og-ra-pher
cho-re-og-ra-phy
cho-ris-ter
cho-rus
chose

cho-sen
chow-der
chris-ten
chrome
chro-mo-some

chronic
chroni-cally
chron-icle
chro-no-log-ical
chro-no-logi-cally

chro-nol-ogy
chry-san-the-mum
chuckle
church
churches

churn-ing
chute
cider
cigar
ciga-rette

ci-gars
cin-der
cin-ema
cine-ma-tog-ra-phy
cin-na-mon

ci-pher
cir-cle
cir-cled
cir-cles
cir-cling

cir-cuit
cir-cuitry
cir-cu-lar
cir-cu-lar-ize
cir-cu-lar-ized

cir-cu-lar-iz-ing
cir-cu-late
cir-cu-lated
cir-cu-lat-ing
cir-cu-la-tion

cir-cu-la-tory
cir-cum-fer-ence
cir-cum-fer-en-tial
cir-cum-flex
cir-cum-scribe

cir-cum-spect
cir-cum-stance
cir-cum-stances
cir-cum-stan-tial
cir-cum-vent

cir-cum-vented
cir-cus
ci-ta-tion
cite
cited

cit-ies
cit-ing
citi-zen
citi-zenry
citi-zen-ship

cit-rus
city
civic
civ-ics
civil

ci-vil-ian
civi-li-za-tion
civi-lize
civi-lized
claim

claim-able
claim-ant
claimed
claim-ing
clair-voy-ance

clair-voy-ant
clamor
clam-or-ing
clamp
clamp-ing

clan-des-tine
clari-fi-ca-tion
clari-fied
clari-fier
clari-fies

clar-ify
clari-fy-ing
clari-net
clar-ity
class

classed
classes
clas-sic
clas-si-cal
clas-si-fi-ca-tion

clas-si-fied
clas-sify
clas-si-fy-ing
class-mate
class-room

class-work
clause
clauses
claw-back
clean

cleaned
cleaner
clean-ers
clean-est
clean-ing

clean-li-ness
cleanly
cleansed
cleanser
cleanup

clear
clear-ance
clear-ances
cleared
clearer

clear-ing
clearing-house
clearly
clear-ness
cleav-age

cleaver
clem-ency
clem-ent
clergy
cler-ical

clerk
clever
cli•ché
cli•ent
cli-en-tele

cli-mate
cli-ma-to-log-ical
cli•max
climb
climb-ing

clinic
clin-ical
clini-cally
cli-ni-cian
clin-ics

clip
clipped
clip-per
clip-ping
cloak

cloak-room
clob-ber
clock
clock-ing
clock-wise

clock-work
clogged
clois-ter
close
closed

closely
close-ness
close-out
closer
closes

clos-est
closet
clos-ets
clos-ing
clo-sure

cloth
clothes
cloth-ing
cloud
cloud-burst

clouded
cloudy
clout
clo•ver
clover-leaf

clown-ish
club
club-foot
club-house
clue

clum-si-ness
clumsy
clus-ter
clutch
clutched

clutches
clut-ter
clut-tered
coach
coached

coaches
coach-ing
co•ad-justor
co•agu-lant
co•agu-late

co•agu-la-tion
coal
co•ali-tion
co--applicant
coarse

coarser
coast
coastal
coaster
coast-ing

coat
coated
coat-ing
co•au-thor
coax

co•ax-ial
cob
co•balt
cob-bler
cobble-stone

cob•web
cock-pit
cock-roach
cock-tail
co•co-nut

cod•dle
cod-dling
code
coded
co•de-fen-dant

codi-cil
codi-fied
cod•ing
co--director
coed

co•edu-ca-tion
co•ef-fi-cient
co•erce
co•er-cion
co•ex-ist

co•ex-is-tence
co--facilitate
cof•fee
coffer•dam
cof-fers

cof•fin
co--founder
co•gent
cogi-tate
cogi-ta-tion

cog-ni-tive
cog-ni-zance
cog-ni-zant
co•here
co•her-ence

co•her-ent
co•he-sion
co•he-sive
co•hort
co•host

co-hosted
coil
coiled
coin
co•in-cide

co•in-cided
co•in-ci-dence
co•in-ci-dent
co•in-ci-den•tal
co•in-ci-den-tally

co•in-cid•ing
co•in-sur-ance
cold
colder
cold-est

co--leader
cole-slaw
coli-seum
co•li-tis
col-labo-rate

col-labo-rated
col-labo-ra-tion
col-labo-ra•tor
col-labo-ra-tive
col-labo-ra-tively

col-lage
col-lapse
col-lapsed
col-laps-ible
col-laps•ing

col•lar
col-late
col-lated
col-lat-eral
col-lat•ing

col-la•tor
col-league
col-lect
col-lected
col-lecti-bil•ity

col-lect-ible
col-lect•ing
col-lec-tion
col-lec-tive
col-lec-tively

col-lec•tor
col-lege
col-leges
col-le-gian
col-le-giate

col-lide
col-lided
col-li-sion
col•lo-quial
col•lo-qui-al•ism

col•lo-quium
col-lo•quy
col-lude
col-lu-sion
col-lu-sive

co•logne
colon
colo-nel
co•lo-nial
colo-nies

colo-nize
col•ony
color
Colo-rado
col-or-ation

color--bearer
color--blind
col-ored
color-fast
col•or-ful

col•or-ing
col•or-less
col•ors
co•los-sal
col-os-seum

co•los-sus
co•los-tomy
col-por-teur
col•umn
co•lum-nar

col-um-nist
com•bat
com-bat•ant
com-bat•ing
combed

com-bi-na-tion
com-bine
com-bined
comb-ing
com-bin•ing

combo
com-bus-ti•ble
com-bus-tion
come
come-back

co•me-dian
come-dies
com•edy
come-li-ness
comely

come--on
comet
com-fort
com-fort-able
com-fort-ably

com-forter
com-fort•ing
comic
com-ical
com•ing

comma
com-mand
com-man-dant
com-mander
com-mand•ing

com-mand-ment
com-memo-rate
com-memo-rated
com-memo-rat•ing
com-memo-ra-tive

com-mence
com-menced
com-mence-ment
com-mences
com-menc•ing

com-mend
com-mend-able
com-men-da-tion
com-men-da-tory
com-mended

com-mend•ing
com-men-su-rate
com-ment
com-men-tar•ies
com-men-tary

com-men-ta•tor
com-mented
com-ment•ing
com-merce
com-mer-cial

com-mer-cial•ism
com-mer-cial-iza-tion
com-mer-cial•ize
com-mer-cial-ized
com-mer-cially

com-min•gle
com-mis-er•ate
com-mis-sar•ies
com-mis-sary
com-mis-sion

com-mis-sioned
com-mis-sioner
com-mis-sion•ing
com•mit
com-mit-ment

com-mit•ted
com-mit•tee
com•mit-ting
com-mode
com-modi-ties

com-mod•ity
com-mo-dore
com•mon
com-mon•est
com-monly

common-place
common-wealth
com-mo-tion
com-mu•nal
com-mune

com-mu-ni-ca•ble
com-mu-ni-cate
com-mu-ni-cated
com-mu-ni-cat•ing
com-mu-ni-ca-tion

com-mu-ni-ca-tive
com-mu-ni-ca-tively
com-mu-ni-ca•tor
com-mu-ni•qué
com-mu-nism

com-mu-nist
com-mu-nis•tic
com-mu-ni-ties
com-mu-nity
com-mu-tate

com-mu-ta-tion
com-mute
com-muter
com-mut•ing
com-pact

com-pact•ing
com-pactly
com-pact-ness
com-pac•tor
com-pa-nies

com-pan·ion
com-pan·ion-ship
com-pany
com-pa-ra-bil·ity
com-pa-ra·ble

com-para-tive
com-para-tively
com-pare
com-pared
com-par·ing

com-pari·son
com-part-ment
com-part-men-tal·ize
com-pass
com-pas-sion

com-pas-sion·ate
com-pati-bil·ity
com-pat-ible
com·pel
com-pelled

com-pel-ling
com-pen-sa·ble
com-pen-sate
com-pen-sated
com-pen-sat·ing

com-pen-sa-tion
com-pen-sa-tory
com-pete
com-pe-tence
com-pe-ten-cies

com-pe-tency
com-pe-tent
com-pe-tently
com-pet·ing
com-pe-ti-tion

com-peti-tive
com-peti-tively
com-peti-tive-ness
com-peti·tor
com-pi-la-tion

com-pile
com-piled
com-piler
com-pil·ing
com-pla-cence

com-pla-cency
com-pla-cent
com-plain
com-plain·ant
com-plained

com-plain·ing
com-plaint
com-plai-sance
com-plai-sant
com-ple-ment

com-ple-men-tary
com-ple-mented
com-plete
com-pleted
com-pletely

com-plete-ness
com-plet·ing
com-ple-tion
com-plex
com-plexes

com-plex·ion
com-plexi-ties
com-plex·ity
com-pli-ance
com-pli-cate

com-pli-cated
com-pli-cat·ing
com-pli-ca-tion
com-plied
com-plies

com-pli-ment
com-pli-men-tary
com-pli-mented
com·ply
com-ply·ing

com-po-nent
com-port-ment
com-pose
com-posed
com-poser

com-pos·ing
com-pos·ite
com-po-si-tion
com-post
com-po-sure

com-pound
com-pounded
com-pound·ing
com-pre-hend
com-pre-hen-si·ble

com-pre-hen-sion
com-pre-hen-sive
com-pre-hen-sively
com-press
com-pressed

com-press-ible
com-pres-sion
com-pres-sive
com-pres·sor
com-prise

com-prised
com-prises
com-pro-mise
com-pro-mised
com-pro-mis·ing

comp-trol·ler
com-pul-sion
com-pul-sive
com-pul-sory
com-punc-tion

com-pu-ta-tion
com-pu-ta-tional
com-pute
com-puted
com-puter

com-put-er-iza-tion
com-put-er•ize
com-put-er-ized
com-put-er-iz•ing
com-put•ing

com-rade
con-cave
con-ceal
con-cealed
con-ceal-ment

con-cede
con-ceit
con-ceited
con-ceiv-able
con-ceiv-ably

con-ceive
con-ceived
con-cen-trate
con-cen-trated
con-cen-trat•ing

con-cen-tra-tion
con-cept
con-cep-tion
con-cep-tual
con-cep-tu-al•ize

con-cep-tu-al-iz•ing
con-cep-tu-ally
con-cern
con-cerned
con-cern•ing

con-cert
con-certed
concert-master
con-ces-sion
con-ces-sional

con-cili•ate
con-cili-ation
con-cili-ator
con-cil-ia-tory
con-cise

con-cisely
con-clave
con-clude
con-cluded
con-clud•ing

con-clu-sion
con-clu-sive
con-clu-sively
con-coct
con-coc-tion

con-comi-tant
con-cord
con-cor-dance
con-cor-dant
con-course

con-crete
con•cur
con-curred
con-cur-rence
con-cur-rent

con-cur-rently
con-cur-ring
con-cus-sion
con-demn
con-dem-na-tion

con-demned
con-demn•ing
con-den-sate
con-den-sa-tion
con-dense

con-densed
con-denser
con-dens•ing
con-de-scend
con-de-scend•ing

con-de-scen-sion
con-di-ment
con-di-tion
con-di-tional
con-di-tion-ally

con-di-tioned
con-di-tioner
con-di-tion•ing
con-dole
con-do-lence

con-do-min•ium
con-done
con-doned
con-du-cive
con-duct

con-ducted
con-duct-ibil•ity
con-duct-ible
con-duct•ing
con-duc-tion

con-duc-tive
con-duc•tor
con-duit
con-fabu-late
con-fabu-la-tion

con-fec-tion
con-fec-tioner
con-fec-tion•ery
con-fed-er•acy
con-fed-er•ate

con-fed-era-tion
con•fer
con-feree
con-fer-ence
con-fer-ences

con-fer•ral
con-ferred
con-fer-ring
con-fess
con-fessed

con-fes-sion
con-fetti
con-fi-dant
con-fide
con-fi-dence

con-fi-dent
con-fi-den-tial
con-fi-den-ti-al•ity
con-fi-den-tially
con-fi-dently

con-fid•ing
con-figu-ra-tion
con-fine
con-fined
con-fine-ment

con-fin•ing
con-firm
con-fir-ma-tion
con-fir-ma-tory
con-firmed

con-firm•ing
con-fis-cate
con-fis-ca-tion
con-fis-ca-tory
con-flict

con-flicted
con-flict•ing
con-flu-ence
con-flu•ent
con-form

con-form-able
con-for-mance
con-for-ma-tion
con-formed
con-form•ing

con-form•ist
con-for-mity
con-founded
con-front
con-fron-ta-tion

con-fronted
con-front•ing
con-fuse
con-fused
con-fuses

con-fus•ing
con-fu-sion
con-ge-nial
con-geni-tal
con-gest

con-gested
con-ges-tion
con-ges-tive
con-glom-er-ate
con-glom-era-tion

con-gratu-late
con-gratu-lated
con-gratu-lat•ing
con-gratu-la-tions
con-gratu-la-tory

con-gre-gate
con-gre-gated
con-gre-gat•ing
con-gre-ga-tion
con-gre-ga-tional

con-gress
con-gres-sio•nal
con-gru-ence
con-gru•ent
con-gru•ity

con-gru•ous
con-jec-tural
con-jec-ture
con-ju-gate
con-ju-ga-tion

con-junc-tion
con-junc-ti•val
con-junc-tive
con-jured
con-nect

con-nected
Con-necti-cut
con-nect•ing
con-nec-tion
con-nec•tor

con-nive
con-no-ta-tion
con-no-ta-tive
con-note
con-quer

con-quered
con-quer•ing
con-queror
con-quest
con-science

con-sci-en-tious
con-sci-en-tiously
con-scious
con-scious-ness
con-se-crate

con-se-crated
con-se-cra-tion
con-secu-tive
con-secu-tively
con-sen•sus

con-sent
con-sented
con-sent•ing
con-se-quence
con-se-quences

con-se-quent
con-se-quen-tial
con-se-quently
con-ser-va-tion
con-ser-va-tion•ist

con-ser-va-tism
con-ser-va-tive
con-ser-va-tively
con-ser-va-tory
con-serve

con-served
con-serv•ing
con-sider
con-sid-er-able
con-sid-er-ably

con-sid-er•ate
con-sid-er-ation
con-sid-ered
con-sid-er•ing
con-sid•ers

con-sign
con-signed
con-signee
con-sign•ing
con-sign-ment

con-signor
con-sist
con-sisted
con-sis-tence
con-sis-tency

con-sis-tent
con-sis-tently
con-sist•ing
con-so-la-tion
con-sole

con-soli-date
con-soli-dated
con-soli-dat•ing
con-soli-da-tion
con-so-nance

con-so-nant
con-sort
con-sor•tia
con-sor-tium
con-spicu•ous

con-spicu-ously
con-spir•acy
con-spira•tor
con-spire
con-spired

con-sta•ble
con-stancy
con-stant
con-stantly
con-stel-la-tion

con-ster-na-tion
con-sti-pate
con-sti-pa-tion
con-stitu-ency
con-stitu•ent

con-sti-tute
con-sti-tuted
con-sti-tut•ing
con-sti-tu-tion
con-sti-tu-tional

con-sti-tu-tion-al•ity
con-strain
con-strained
con-straint
con-strict

con-stricted
con-struct
con-structed
con-struct•ing
con-struc-tion

con-struc-tive
con-struc-tively
con-struc•tor
con-strue
con•sul

con-sular
con-sul•ate
con-sult
con-sul-tant
con-sul-ta-tion

con-sul-ta-tive
con-sulted
con-sult•ing
con-sum-able
con-sume

con-sumed
con-sumer
con-sum•ers
con-sum•ing
con-sum-mate

con-sum-mated
con-sump-tion
con-tact
con-tacted
con-tact•ing

con-ta-gion
con-ta-gious
con-tain
con-tained
con-tainer

con-tain-er-iza-tion
con-tain-er-ized
con-tain•ers
con-tain•ing
con-tain-ment

con-tami-nant
con-tami-nate
con-tami-nated
con-tami-nat•ing
con-tami-na-tion

con-tem-plate
con-tem-plated
con-tem-plat•ing
con-tem-pla-tion
con-tem-pla-tive

con-tem-po-ra-ne•ous
con-tem-po-ra-ne-ously
con-tem-po-rar•ies
con-tem-po-rary
con-tempt

con-tempt-ible
con-temp-tu•ous
con-tend
con-tended
con-tender

con-tend•ing
con-tent
con-tented
con-ten-tion
con-tent-ment

con-test
con-test-able
con-tes-tant
con-tested
con-test•ing

con-text
con-tex-tual
con-ti-gu•ity
con-tigu•ous
con-ti-nence

con-ti-nent
con-ti-nen•tal
con-tin-gen-cies
con-tin-gency
con-tin-gent

con-tinu-able
con-tin•ual
con-tinu-ally
con-tinu-ance
con-tinu-ances

con-tinu-ation
con-tinue
con-tin•ued
con-tin•ues
con-tinu•ing

con-ti-nu-ities
con-ti-nu•ity
con-tinu•ous
con-tinu-ously
con-tort

con-tor-tion
con-tor-tion•ist
con-tour
con-tra-band
con-tract

con-tracted
con-tract-ible
con-tract•ing
con-trac-tion
con-trac•tor

con-trac-tual
con-tra-dict
con-tra-dicted
con-tra-dic-tion
con-tra-dic-tory

con-trary
con-trast
con-trasted
con-trast•ing
con-tra-vene

con-tra-ven-tion
con-trib•ute
con-trib-uted
con-trib-ut•ing
con-tri-bu-tion

con-tribu•tor
con-tribu-tory
con-trite
con-triv-ance
con-trive

con-trived
con-trol
con-trol-la•ble
con-trolled
con-trol•ler

con-trol-ling
con-tro-ver-sial
con-tro-versy
con-tuse
con-tu-sion

con-va-lesce
con-va-les-cence
con-va-les-cent
con-va-lesc•ing
con-vene

con-vened
con-ve-nience
con-ve-niences
con-ve-nient
con-ve-niently

con-ven•ing
con-vent
con-ven-tion
con-ven-tional
con-verge

con-ver-sant
con-ver-sa-tion
con-ver-sa-tional
con-verse
con-versed

con-versely
con-ver-sion
con-vert
con-verted
con-verter

con-vert•ers
con-vert-ibil•ity
con-vert-ible
con-vert•ing
con•vex

con-vex•ity
con•vey
con-vey-ance
con-veyed
con-vey•ing

con-veyor
con-vict
con-vic-tion
con-vince
con-vinced

con-vinces
con-vinc•ing
con-vinc-ingly
con-vo-ca-tion
con•voy

con-vul-sion
con-vul-sive
cook
cooked
cook-ery

cook-ies
cook-ing
cook-out
cook-ware
cool

cool-ant
cooled
cooler
cool-ing
coop

co--op
co•op-er•ate
co•op-er-ated
co•op-er-at•ing
co•op-era-tion

co•op-era-tive
co•op-era-tively
co•op-era-tive-ness
co•or-di-nate
co•or-di-nated

co•or-di-nat•ing
co•or-di-na-tion
co•or-di-na•tor
co--owner
cop

co•pay-ment
cope
cop•ied
copier
cop•ies

co•pi-lot
cop•ing
cop•per
copy
copy-holder

copy-ing
copy-right
copy-righted
copy-writer
cord

cord-board
cor-dial
cor-dial•ity
cor-dially
cord-less

cor-du•roy
core
core-less
corn
cor•nea

cor•ner
cor-nered
cor-ner•ing
corner-stone
cor•net

cor-nu-co•pia
cor-ol-lary
co•rona
coro-nar•ies
coro-nary

coro-na-tion
coro-ner
coro-net
cor-po•ral
cor-po-rate

cor-po-ra-tion
corps
corpse
cor•pus
cor-pus•cle

cor•ral
cor-rect
cor-rected
cor-rect•ing
cor-rec-tion

cor-rec-tional
cor-rec-tive
cor-rectly
cor-rect-ness
cor-re-late

cor-re-lated
cor-re-lat•ing
cor-re-la-tion
cor-re-spond
cor-re-sponded

cor-re-spon-dence
cor-re-spon-dent
cor-re-spond•ing
cor-re-spond-ingly
cor-ri•dor

cor-ri-gi•ble
cor-robo-rate
cor-robo-rated
cor-robo-rat•ing
cor-robo-ra-tion

cor-rode
cor-roded
cor-rod•ing
cor-ro-sion
cor-ru-gate

cor-ru-gated
cor-ru-ga-tion
cor-rupt
cor-rupt-ible
cor-rup-tion

cor-sage
cor-ti•cal
co•se-cant
co•signer
cos-metic

cos-met•ics
cos-me-tol•ogy
cos•mic
cos-mo-poli•tan
cos•mos

co•spon-sor
co•spon-sored
co•spon-sor-ship
cost
cost-ing

costly
cos-tume
cot-tage
cot-tages
cot•ton

cou•gar
cough
could
couldn't
coun-cil

coun-cilor
coun-sel
coun-seled
coun-sel•ing
coun-selor

coun-sel•ors
count
count-down
counted
counter

coun-ter•act
coun-ter-bal-ance
coun-ter-bal-anced
coun-ter-bal-anc•ing
coun-ter-clock-wise

coun-tered
coun-ter-feit
coun-ter•ing
coun-ter-in-tel-li-gence
coun-ter-mand

coun-ter-part
coun-ter-pro-duc-tive
coun-ter-signed
coun-ter-sued
counter-top

coun-ties
count-ing
count-less
coun-tries
coun-try

county
cou•ple
cou-pled
cou-pler
cou-pling

cou•pon
cour-age
cou-ra-geous
cou-rier
course

coursed
courses
course-work
court
cour-te•ous

cour-te-ously
cour-te-sies
cour-tesy
court-house
court-ing

court--martial
court-room
cousin
co•va-lently
cove-nant

cover
cov-er•age
cov-er-ages
cov-er-alls
cov-ered

cov-er•ing
cov•ers
co•vert
co•vertly
co•vert-ness

covet
cov-et•ous
cow•ard
cow-ard•ice
co--worker

cow-poke
coy•ote
crack
crack-down
cracked

cracker
crack-ing
crackle
cra•dle
craft

crafts-man-ship
crammed
cramped
crane
cra-nial

cra-ni-ome•try
crank-case
crank-shaft
crash
crashed

crashes
crash-ing
crash-worthiness
crash-worthy
crated

cra•ter
crat-ing
crav-ing
crawl
crawl-ing

crayon
cray•ons
crazy
cream
creamer

cream-ery
creamy
cre•ate
cre-ated
cre-at•ing

cre-ation
cre-ative
cre-atively
cre-ativ•ity
cre-ator

crea-ture
cre-dence
cre-den-tial
credi-bil•ity
cred-ible

credit
cred-it-able
cred-ited
cred-it•ing
credi-tor

credu-lous
creed
creek
creep
creep-ing

cre-ma-tion
creo-sote
creo-soted
cres-cent
crest

crew
cried
cries
crime
crimi-nal

crimi-nal•ity
crimi-nol•ogy
crimp
crimped
crimp-ing

crim-son
crip-ple
crip-pled
crip-pling
cri•ses

cri•sis
cri-te•ria
cri-te-rion
critic
crit-ical

criti-cally
criti-cism
criti-cize
criti-cized
criti-ciz•ing

crit-ics
cri-tique
crock-ery
croco-dile
crook

crooked
crop
cro-quet
cross
cross-bar

crossed
crosses
cross-ing
cross--reference
cross-road

cross-walk
cross-wise
cro•ton
crowd
crowded

crowd-ing
crown
crowned
cru-cial
cru-ci•fix

crude
cruel
cru-elty
cruise
cruises

crum-ble
crum-bled
crum-bling
crunch
cru-sade

cru-sader
crush
crushed
crusher
crush-ing

crust
crutch
crutches
cry
cry•ing

cryp-tic
cryp-to-logic
crys-tal
crys-tal-lize
crys-tal-liz•ing

cub•age
cube
cubic
cu•cum-ber
cui-sine

cul--de--sac
cu•li-nary
cul-mi-nate
cul-mi-nated
cul-mi-nat•ing

cul-mi-na-tion
cul-prit
cul-ti-vate
cul-ti-vated
cul-ti-va-tion

cul-tural
cul-tur-ally
cul-ture
cul-tured
cul-vert

cum-ber-some
cu·mu-la-tive
cun-ning
cun-ningly
cup

cup-board
cur-able
cu·ra-tor
curb
curbed

curb-ing
cure
cured
cur·few
cur·ing

cu·ri-os·ity
cu·ri-ous
curled
curler
cur-ren-cies

cur-rency
cur-rent
cur-rently
cur-ric·ula
cur-ricu·lar

cur-ricu·lum
curse
cur-sive
cur-sory
cur-tail

cur-tailed
cur-tail-ment
cur-tain
curtsy
cur-va-ture

curve
curved
cush-ion
cush-ioned
cush-ion·ing

cus-tard
cus-to-dial
cus-to-dian
cus-tody
cus·tom

cus-tom-arily
cus-tom·ary
cus-tomer
cus-tom·ers
cut

cut-back
cu·ti-cle
cut-lery
cut·off
cut·ter

cut-ting
cy·ber-net·ics
cycle
cy·cled
cy·cles

cy·cli-cal
cy·clone
cyl-in·der
cym·bal
cyn-ical

cyni-cism

_D_

daf-fo·dil
dai-lies
daily
dair-ies
dairy

dam·age
dam-aged
dam-ages
dam-ag·ing
dam·ask

damp
dampen
damp-ened
damp-ness
dance

dancer
dances
danc-ing
dan-de-lion
dan-druff

dandy
dan·ger
dan-ger·ous
dan-ger-ously
dan·gle

dan-gling
dare
dar·ing
dark
darker

dark-ness
dark-room
dar-ling
dash
dashed

data
data base
data bases
data links
data set

date
dated
dat·ing
datum
daugh-ter

dav-en-port
dawn
dawned
day
day-dream

day-dreaming
day-light
day-time
daz·zle
de·ac·ti·vate

dead
dead-beat
deaden
dead-line
dead-lock

deadly
deaf
deafen
deaf-en·ing
deaf-ness

deal
dealer
deal-ers
deal-er-ship
deal-ing

dealt
dean
dear
dearly
death

death-less
deathly
de·ba·cle
de·bat-able
de·bate

de·bated
de·bat-ing
de·ben-ture
de·bili-tate
de·bili-tated

debit
deb-ited
deb·its
debo-nair
de·bris

debt
debtor
de·bug-ging
de·cade
deca-dence

deca-dent
decal
de·cals
de·cant
de·cath-lon

decay
de·cease
de·ceased
de·ce-dent
de·ceit

de·ceit-ful
de·ceive
de·ceived
de·ceiv-ing
de·cel-er·ate

de·cel-era-tion
de·cel-era-tive
De·cem-ber
de·cency
de·cent

de·cen-tral·ize
de·cen-tral-ized
de·cen-tral-iz·ing
de·cep-tion
de·cep-tive

deci-bel
de·cide
de·cided
de·cid-edly
de·cid-ing

deci-mal
de·ci-pher
de·ci-sion
de·ci-sional
de·ci-sive

de·ci-sively
deck
dec-la-ra-tion
de·clara-tive
de·clara-tory

de·clare
de·clared
de·clar-ing
de·clas-sify
dec-li-na-tion

de·cline
de·clined
de·clin-ing
de·com-pose
de·com-press

de·con-ges-tant
de·con-tami-nate
de·con-trol
de·con-trolled
decor

deco-rate
deco-rated
deco-rat·ing
deco-ra-tion
deco-ra-tive

deco-ra·tor
de·co-rum
de·crease
de·creased
de·creases

de·creas-ing
de·cree
de·creed
de·crimi-nal-iza-tion
dedi-cate

dedi-cated
dedi-cat·ing
dedi-ca-tion
dedi-ca-tory
de·duce

D

de•duc-ible
de•duct
de•ducted
de•duct-ibil•ity
de•duct-ible

de•duct-ing
de•duc-tion
deed
deeded
deem

deemed
deep
deepen
deeper
deep-est

deeply
deer
de--escalation
de•face
de•fac-ing

de•fal-cate
de•fal-ca-tion
defa-ma-tion
de•fama-tory
de•fault

de•faulted
de•fault-ing
de•feat
de•feated
de•feat-ist

de•fect
de•fec-tive
de•fend
de•fen-dant
de•fended

de•fender
de•fend-ing
de•fense
de•fenses
de•fen-si•ble

de•fen-sive
de•fen-sively
defer
def-er-ence
de•fer-ment

de•fer-ral
de•ferred
de•fer-ring
de•fi-ance
de•fi-ant

de•fi-cien-cies
de•fi-ciency
de•fi-cient
defi-cit
de•fies

de•fin-able
de•fine
de•fined
de•fin-ing
defi-nite

defi-nitely
defi-ni-tion
de•fini-tive
de•fini-tively
de•flate

de•fla-tion
de•fla-tor
de•flect
de•flec-tion
defog

de•fo-li•ant
de•fo-li•ate
de•fo-li-ated
de•form
de•for-ma-tion

de•formed
de•form-ing
de•for-mity
de•fraud
de•fraud-ing

de•fray
de•frost
de•frosted
de•froster
de•funct

de•fuse
de•gen-er•ate
de•gen-era-tion
deg-ra-da-tion
de•grade

de•graded
de•greaser
de•greas-ing
de•gree
de•hu-midi-fi-ca-tion

de•hy-drated
de•hy-drat-ing
de•jected
de•jec-tion
Dela-ware

delay
de•layed
de•lay-ing
de•lec-ta•ble
dele-gate

dele-gated
dele-ga-tion
de•lete
de•leted
dele-te-ri•ous

de•let-ing
de•le-tion
de•lib-er•ate
de•lib-er-ately
de•lib-er-at•ing

deli-cacy
deli-cate
deli-ca-tes•sen
de•li-cious
de•light

de·lighted
de·light-ful
de·light-fully
de·lin-eate
de·lin-eated

de·lin-eat·ing
de·lin-ea-tion
de·lin-quen-cies
de·lin-quency
de·lin-quent

de·liri-ous
de·lir-ium
de·liver
de·liv-er-able
de·liv-er-ance

de·liv-ered
de·liv-er·ies
de·liv-er·ing
de·liv-ery
delta

de·lude
de·luded
del·uge
del-uged
de·lu-sion

de·luxe
delve
delv-ing
de·mand
de·manded

de·mand-ing
de·mar-cate
de·mean
de·meanor
de·mented

de·men-tia
de·merit
de·mise
demo
de·mo-bi-li-za-tion

de·mo-bi-lize
de·moc-racy
demo-crat
demo-cratic
de·mo-graphic

de·mog-ra·phy
de·mol-ish
de·mol-ished
de·mol-ish·ing
de·mo-li-tion

de·mon-stra·ble
de·mon-stra·bly
dem-on-strate
dem-on-strated
dem-on-strat·ing

dem-on-stra-tion
de·mon-stra-tive
dem-on-stra·tor
de·mor-al·ize
de·mote

de·mo-tion
de·mount
de·mount-able
de·mur-rage
de·nial

de·nied
de·nier
de·nies
denim
den·ims

de·nomi-na-tion
de·nomi-na-tional
de·nomi-na·tor
de·note
de·noted

de·not-ing
de·nounce
dense
den-si-fied
den-sity

den·tal
dented
den-ti-frice
den-tist
den-tistry

den-ture
deny
de·ny-ing
de·odor-ant
de·odor-ize

de·odor-izer
de·part
de·parted
de·part-ing
de·part-ment

de·part-men·tal
de·part-men-tal·ize
de·par-ture
de·pend
de·pend-abil·ity

de·pend-able
de·pended
de·pen-dence
de·pen-dency
de·pen-dent

de·pend-ing
de·pict
de·picted
de·pict-ing
de·plete

de·pleted
de·ple-tion
de·plor-able
de·plore
de·ploy

de·ployed
de·ploy-ment
de·popu-late
de·popu-la-tion
de·port

de·por·ta·tion
de·port·ment
de·pose
de·poses
de·posit

de·pos·ited
de·pos·it·ing
de·po·si·tion
de·posi·tor
de·posi·to·ries

de·posi·tory
depot
de·pre·cia·ble
de·pre·ci·ate
de·pre·ci·ated

de·pre·cia·tion
de·press
de·pres·sant
de·pressed
de·press·ing

de·pres·sion
de·pri·va·tion
de·prive
de·prived
depth

depu·ties
depu·tize
dep·uty
de·rail·ment
de·regu·la·tion

de·regu·la·tive
deri·va·tion
de·riva·tive
de·rive
de·rived

de·riv·ing
der·ma·tolo·gist
der·ma·tol·ogy
der·ma·to·logic
de·roga·tory

de·scend
de·scen·dant
de·scend·ing
de·scent
de·scribe

de·scribed
de·scrib·ing
de·scrip·tion
de·scrip·tive
de·scrip·tor

de·sea·son·al·ized
de·seg·re·gate
de·seg·re·ga·tion
de·sert (v.)
de·serted

de·ser·tion
de·serve
de·served
de·serv·ing
de·sign

des·ig·nate
des·ig·nated
des·ig·nat·ing
des·ig·na·tion
de·signed

des·ig·nee
de·signer
de·sign·ers
de·sign·ing
de·sir·abil·ity

de·sir·able
de·sire
de·sired
de·sir·ing
de·sir·ous

de·sist
desk
deso·late
deso·la·tion
de·spair

des·per·ate
des·per·ately
des·pera·tion
de·spi·ca·ble
de·spise

de·spite
de·spite·ful
de·spon·dence
de·spon·dent
des·sert

de·stig·ma·ti·za·tion
des·ti·na·tion
des·tined
des·tiny
des·ti·tute

de·stroy
de·stroyed
de·stroyer
de·stroy·ing
de·struct

de·struc·ti·bil·ity
de·struc·ti·ble
de·struc·tion
de·struc·tive
de·tach

de·tached
de·tach·ment
de·tail
de·tailed
de·tail·ing

de·tain
de·tainer
de·tain·ing
de·tect
de·tect·able

de·tected
de·tect·ing
de·tec·tion
de·tec·tive
de·tec·tor

de-ten-tion
deter
de-ter-gent
de-te-rio-rate
de-te-rio-rated

de-te-rio-rat-ing
de-te-rio-ra-tion
de-ter-mi-nant
de-ter-mi-na-tion
de-ter-mine

de-ter-mined
de-ter-min-ing
de-terred
de-ter-rent
de-test

de-test-able
deto-nate
deto-na-tion
deto-na-tor
de-tour

de-tract
de-tracted
de-trac-tion
det-ri-ment
det-ri-men-tal

de-valu-ate
de-valu-ation
dev-as-tate
dev-as-tated
dev-as-tat-ing

dev-as-ta-tion
de-velop
de-vel-oped
de-vel-oper
de-vel-op-ing

de-vel-op-ment
de-vel-op-men-tal
de-vel-op-men-tally
de-vi-ate
de-via-tion

de-vice
de-vices
dev-il-ish
de-vi-ous
de-vise

de-vised
de-vises
de-void
de-vote
de-voted

de-vot-ing
de-vo-tion
de-vo-tional
de-vour
de-vout

dex-ter-ity
dex-ter-ous
dex-trose
dia-be-tes
dia-betic

dia-bolic
di-ag-nose
di-ag-nosed
di-ag-nos-tic
di-ag-nos-ti-cian

di-ago-nal
dia-gram
dia-gram-matic
dia-grammed
dial

dia-lect
di-aled
di-aler
di-al-ing
dia-logue

di-aly-sis
di-ame-ter
dia-met-ric
dia-met-ri-cal
dia-mond

dia-per
dia-phragm
di-ar-rhea
diary
diced

di-chot-omy
dic-tate
dic-tated
dic-tat-ing
dic-ta-tion

dic-ta-tor
dic-tion
dic-tio-nar-ies
dic-tio-nary
did

didn't
die
died
die-sel
diet

di-etary
di-etetic
di-eti-tian
dif-fer
dif-fered

dif-fer-ence
dif-fer-ences
dif-fer-ent
dif-fer-en-tial
dif-fer-en-ti-ate

dif-fer-en-tia-tion
dif-fer-ently
dif-fer-ing
dif-fi-cult
dif-fi-cul-ties

dif-fi-culty
dif-fuse
dif-fused
dif-fuser
dif-fus-ing

dig
di•gest
di•gested
di•gest-ing
di•ges-tive

dig•ger
dig-ging
digit
digi-tal
dig-ni-fied

dig-nify
dig-ni-tar•ies
dig-ni-tary
dig-nity
di•gress

di•gres-sion
dike
di•lapi-dated
di•lapi-da-tion
dila-tory

di•lemma
dili-gence
dili-gent
dili-gently
di•lute

di•luted
di•lu-tion
dime
di•men-sion
di•men-sional

di•min-ish
di•min-ished
di•min-ish•ing
dimi-nu-tion
dimly

dim•mer
diner
di•ners
di•nette
dingy

din•ing
din•ner
din-ner-ware
di•no-saur
di•oce-san

dio-cese
dio-ceses
diode
di•orama
di•ox-ide

diph-the•ria
diph-thong
di•ploma
di•plo-macy
di•plo-mas

dip-lo•mat
dip-lo-matic
dip-lo-mati-cally
dipped
dip•per

dip-ping
di•rect
di•rected
di•rect-ing
di•rec-tion

di•rec-tional
di•rec-tive
di•rectly
di•rec-tor
di•rec-tor•ate

di•rec-to-ries
di•rec-tor-ship
di•rec-tory
dirt
dirty

dis-abili-ties
dis-abil•ity
dis-able
dis-abled
dis-abling

dis-ad-van-tage
dis-ad-van-taged
dis-ad-van-tages
dis-af-fected
dis-agree

dis-agree-able
dis-agreed
dis-agree-ment
dis-al•low
dis-al-low-ance

dis-al-lowed
dis-ap-pear
dis-ap-pear-ance
dis-ap-peared
dis-ap-pear•ing

dis-ap-point
dis-ap-pointed
dis-ap-point•ing
dis-ap-point-ment
dis-ap-proval

dis-ap-prove
dis•arm
dis-ar-ma-ment
dis-ar•ray
dis-as-sem•ble

dis-as-so-ci•ate
dis-as-so-cia-tion
di•sas-ter
di•sas-trous
dis-band

dis-banded
dis•bar
dis-burse
dis-bursed
dis-burse-ment

dis-burs•ing
dis-card
dis-carded
dis-cern
dis-cerned

dis-cern-ible
dis-cern-ment
dis-charge
dis-charged
dis-charges

dis-charg•ing
dis-ci•ple
dis-ci-pli-nar•ian
dis-ci-plin•ary
dis-ci-pline

dis-ci-plined
dis-ci-plin•ing
dis-claim
dis-claimer
dis-close

dis-closed
dis-closes
dis-clos•ing
dis-clo-sure
disco

dis-color
dis-col-ored
dis-com-fort
dis-con-nect
dis-con-nected

dis-con-nect•ing
dis-con-nec-tion
dis-con-tinu-ance
dis-con-tinue
dis-con-tin•ued

dis-con-tin•ues
dis-con-tinu•ing
dis-con-ti-nu•ity
dis-cord
dis-count

dis-counted
dis-count•ing
dis-cour•age
dis-cour-aged
dis-cour-age-ment

dis-cour-ages
dis-cour-ag•ing
dis-course
dis-cour-tesy
dis-cover

dis-cov-ered
dis-cov-er•ies
dis-cov-er•ing
dis-cov•ery
dis-credit

dis-cred-ited
dis-creet
dis-creetly
dis-crep-an-cies
dis-crep-ancy

dis-crete
dis-cre-tion
dis-cre-tion•ary
dis-crimi-nate
dis-crimi-nat•ing

dis-crimi-na-tion
dis-crimi-na-tive
dis-crimi-na-tory
dis-cuss
dis-cussed

dis-cusses
dis-cuss•ing
dis-cus-sion
dis-ease
dis-eased

dis-eases
dis-fa•vor
dis-fig•ure
dis-fig-ure-ment
dis-func-tional

dis-grace
dis-grace•ful
dis-grun-tled
dis-guise
dis-gust

dis-gusted
dis-heart-en•ing
dishes
di•shevel
dis-hon•est

dis-hon-esty
dis-honor
dis-hon-or-able
dis-hon-ored
dish-washer

dis-il-lu-sion
dis-in-cen-tive
dis-in-fec-tant
dis-in-te-grate
dis-in-te-gra-tion

dis-in-ter-ested
dis-join
dis-junc-tive
disk
dis-like

dis-lo-cate
dis-lo-cat•ing
dis-lo-ca-tion
dis-loyal
dis•mal

dis-man•tle
dis•may
dis-mem•ber
dis-mem-bered
dis-mem-ber-ment

dis-miss
dis-missal
dis-missed
dis-misses
dis-obe-di-ence

dis-obey
dis-or•der
dis-or-derly
dis-or-ga-nize
dis-or-ga-nized

dis-pari-ties
dis-par•ity
dis-patch
dis-patched
dis-patcher

dis-patch•ing
dis•pel
dis-pen-sary
dis-pen-sa-tion
dis-pense

dis-pensed
dis-penser
dis-pens•ing
dis-persal
dis-perse

dis-pers•ing
dis-per-sion
dis-place
dis-placed
dis-place-ment

dis-play
dis-played
dis-player
dis-play•ing
dis-please

dis-plea-sure
dis-pos-able
dis-posal
dis-pose
dis-posed

dis-pos•ing
dis-po-si-tion
dis-pos-sess
dis-pos-sessed
dis-pro-por-tion

dis-pro-por-tional
dis-pro-por-tion•ate
dis-pro-por-tion-ately
dis-prove
dis-pu-ta•ble

dis-pute
dis-puted
dis-put•ing
dis-quali-fi-ca-tion
dis-quali-fied

dis-qual•ify
dis-quali-fy•ing
dis-re-gard
dis-re-garded
dis-re-spect

dis-re-spect•ful
dis-rupt
dis-rupt•ing
dis-rup-tion
dis-rup-tive

dis-sat-is-fac-tion
dis-sat-is-fac-tory
dis-sat-is-fied
dis-sat-isfy
dis-sect

dis-sected
dis-sect•ing
dis-sec-tion
dis-semi-nate
dis-semi-nated

dis-semi-nat•ing
dis-semi-na-tion
dis-sent
dis-ser-ta-tion
dis-ser-vice

dis-simi•lar
dis-si-pate
dis-si-pated
dis-so-lu-tion
dis-solve

dis-solved
dis-solv•ing
dis-so-nance
dis-tance
dis-tances

dis-tant
dis-taste•ful
dis-til-late
dis-tilled
dis-till•ery

dis-tinct
dis-tinc-tion
dis-tinc-tive
dis-tinc-tive-ness
dis-tinctly

dis-tin-guish
dis-tin-guish-able
dis-tin-guished
dis-tin-guish•ing
dis-tort

dis-torted
dis-tor-tion
dis-tract
dis-tract•ing
dis-trac-tion

dis-tress
dis-tressed
dis-tress•ful
dis-tress•ing
dis-trib-ut-able

dis-trib•ute
dis-trib-uted
dis-trib-ut•ing
dis-tri-bu-tion
dis-tribu-tive

dis-tribu•tor
dis-tribu-tor-ship
dis-trict
dis-trust
dis-trust•ful

dis-turb
dis-tur-bance
dis-tur-bances
dis-turbed
dis-turb•ing

dis·use
ditch
ditches
ditto
dive

diver
di·verge
di·ver-gence
di·verg-ing
di·vers

di·verse
di·ver-si-fi-ca-tion
di·ver-si-fied
di·ver-sify
di·ver-sion

di·ver-sity
di·vert
di·verted
di·vert-ing
di·vest

di·vide
di·vided
divi-dend
di·vider
di·vid-ers

di·vid-ing
di·vine
div·ing
di·vin-ity
di·visi-bil·ity

di·vis-ible
di·vi-sion
di·vi-sional
di·vi-sive
di·vi-sive-ness

di·vi-sor
di·vorce
di·vorced
di·vorcée
di·vorces

di·vulge
di·vulged
di·vul-gence
diz-zi-ness
dizzy

do
do·able
doc·ile
dock
docket

dock-eted
dock-ing
doc·tor
doc-toral
doc-tor·ate

doc-trinal
doc-trine
docu-ment
docu-men-tary
docu-men-ta-tion

docu-mented
docu-ment·ing
does
doesn't
dog

dog-matic
doing
dol·lar
dol-phin
do·main

dome
do·mes-tic
do·mes-ti-cally
do·mes-ti-cate
do·mi-cile

do·mi-ciled
do·mi-cili·ary
domi-nance
domi-nant
domi-nate

domi-nated
domi-na-tion
domi-neer·ing
do·min-ion
do·nate

do·nated
do·nat-ing
do·na-tion
done
donor

do·nors
don't
door
door-bell
door-knob

door-way
dor-mant
dor-mi-to-ries
dor-mi-tory
dos·age

dos-ages
dos-sier
dot
dou·ble
dou-bled

dou-bles
dou-bling
dou·bly
doubt
doubted

doubt-ful
doubt-ing
doubt-less
dough-nut
dove-tail

dowel
down
downed
down-grade
down-graded

down-grading
down-hill
down-ing
down-pour
down-right

down-side
down-spout
down-stairs
down-stream
down-swing

down-time
down-town
down-trend
down-turn
down-ward

dozen
doz•ens
draft
drafted
draft-ing

drag
dragged
drag-ging
drag-net
dragon

drain
drain-age
drained
drain-ing
drama

dra-matic
dra-mati-cally
dra-ma-tist
dra-ma-ti-za-tion
dra-ma-tize

dra-ma-tized
drape
draped
drap-er•ies
drap-ery

drap-ing
dras-tic
dras-ti-cally
draw
draw-back

drawer
draw-ers
draw-ing
drawn
dray-age

dread-ful
dream
dreamed
dreamer
dream-ing

dredge
dredg-ing
drenched
dress
dressed

dresser
dress-ers
dresses
dress-ing
drew

dried
drier
drift
drifted
drill

drilled
driller
drill-ing
drink
drinker

drink-ing
drip
dripped
drive
drive--in

driven
driver
driv-ers
drive-way
driv-ing

drool
drool-ing
drop
dropped
drop-ping

drought
drove
drown
drowsy
drudg-ery

drug
drug-gist
drug-store
drum
drum-mer

drunk
drunk-ard
drunken
drunk-en-ness
dry

dryer
dry•ing
dual
du•bi-ous
duct

duc-tile
due
duel
du•el-ist
dues

duet
duf•fel
duly
dummy
dump

dumped
dump-ing
dump-ling
dun-ga•ree
dun-geon

duo-de•nal
duo-de•num
du•plex
du•pli-cate
du•pli-cated

du•pli-cat•ing
du•pli-ca-tion
du•pli-ca-tive
du•pli-ca•tor
du•ra-bil•ity

du•ra-ble
du•ra-tion
du•ress
dur•ing
dusk

dust
dusted
dust-ing
dusty
du•ties

du•ti-ful
duty
dwell
dweller
dwell-ing

dwin-dle
dye
dyed
dye•ing
dyes

dying
dy•namic
dy•nami-cally
dy•nam-ics
dy•na-mite

dy•namo
dy•nasty
dys-func-tion
dys-func-tional

E

each
eager
ea•gerly
eagle
ear

ear-lier
ear-li•est
early
ear-mark
ear-marked

ear-mark•ing
earn
earned
earner
earn-ers

ear-nest
ear-nestly
earn-ing
ear-phone
ear-piece

ear-rings
ear-shot
earth
earth-en-ware
earthly

earth-quake
ease
easel
ease-ment
eas•ier

easi-est
eas•ily
easi-ness
eas•ing
east

east-erly
east-ern
east-ward
east-wardly
easy

easy-going
eat
eat-able
eaten
eat•ing

eaves-drop
ebony
ec•cen-tric
ec•cen-tric•ity
ec•cle-si-as•tic

ec•cle-si-as-ti•cal
eche-lon
echo
echo-ing
eclipse

eco-log-ical
eco-logi-cally
ecolo-gist
ecol-ogy
econo-met-rics

eco-nomic
eco-nom-ical
eco-nomi-cally
eco-nom•ics
econo-mies

econo-mist
econo-mize
econo-mizer
econo-miz•ing
econ-omy

E

ec•stasy
ec•static
ecu-men-ical
ec•zema
edema

edge
edged
edges
edg•ing
ed•ible

edict
edi-fi-ca-tion
edit
ed•ited
ed•it-ing

edi-tion
edi•tor
edi-to-rial
edi-to-ri-al•ize
edi-to-ri-ally

edu-ca•ble
edu-cate
edu-cated
edu-cat•ing
edu-ca-tion

edu-ca-tional
edu-ca-tion-ally
edu-ca-tive
edu-ca•tor
ef•face

ef•fect
ef•fected
ef•fect-ing
ef•fec-tive
ef•fec-tively

ef•fec-tive-ness
ef•fec-tual
ef•fec-tu-ated
ef•fer-ves-cence
ef•fer-ves-cent

ef•fi-ca-cious
ef•fi-ca-ciously
ef•fi-cacy
ef•fi-cien-cies
ef•fi-ciency

ef•fi-cient
ef•fi-ciently
ef•figy
ef•flu-ent
ef•fort

ef•fort-less
ef•fort-lessly
ef•ful-gence
ef•ful-gent
egg

egg•nog
ego-cen-tric
ego•ist
ego-is•tic
ego-is-ti•cal

ego-tism
ego-tist
egress
eight
eigh-teen

eigh-teenth
eighth
eight-ies
eighty
ei•ther

eject
eject-ment
elabo-rate
elabo-rated
elabo-rately

elabo-ra-tion
elapse
elapsed
elas-tic
elas-tic•ity

elated
ela-tion
elbow
elbow-room
elder

el•derly
el•dest
elect
elected
elect-ing

elec-tion
elec-tive
elec-tor
elec-toral
elec-tor•ate

elec•tric
elec-tri•cal
elec-tri-cally
elec-tri-cian
elec-tric•ity

elec-tri-fi-ca-tion
elec-tro-cute
elec-trode
elec-tro-mag-netic
elec-tron

elec-tronic
elec-troni-cally
elec-tron•ics
elec-tro-plat•ing
elec-tro-static

ele-gance
ele-gant
ele-gantly
ele-ment
ele-men•tal

ele-men-tary
ele-phant
ele-vate
ele-vated
ele-vat•ing

ele-va-tion
ele-va•tor
eleven
elev-enth
elicit

elic-ited
elic-it•ing
eli-gi-bil•ity
eli-gi•ble
elimi-nate

elimi-nated
elimi-nat•ing
elimi-na-tion
elite
elk

el-lipse
el•lip-sis
elon-gate
elon-gated
elon-ga-tion

elo-quence
elo-quent
else
else-where
elu-ci-date

elude
elu-sive
ema-nate
eman-ci-pate
em•bank

em•bank-ment
em•bargo
em•bark
em•barked
em•bark-ing

em•bar-rass
em•bar-rassed
em•bar-rass•ing
em•bar-rass-ment
em•bassy

em•bel-lish
ember
em•bez-zle
em•bez-zle-ment
em•blem

em•bod-ied
em•bodi-ment
em•body
em•boss
em•bossed

em•brace
em•braced
em•broi-dery
em•broil
em•broil-ment

em•bryo
em•er-ald
emerge
emerged
emer-gen-cies

emer-gency
emer-gent
emerg-ing
emer-iti
emery

emi-grant
emi-grate
emi-gra-tion
emi-nence
emi-nent

emi-nently
emis-sion
emit
emit-ting
emolu-ment

emo-tion
emo-tional
emo-tion-ally
em•pa-thy
em•pen-nage

em•peror
em•pha-ses
em•pha-sis
em•pha-size
em•pha-sized

em•pha-sizes
em•pha-siz•ing
em•phatic
em•phati-cally
em•phy-sema

em•pire
em•pir-ical
em•ploy
em•ploy-able
em•ployed

em•ployee
em•ployer
em•ploy-ing
em•ploy-ment
em•power

em•pow-ered
emp-tied
emp-ties
empty
emp-ty•ing

emu-late
emul-si-fied
emul-sify
emul-sion
en•able

en•abled
en•abling
enact
en•acted
en•act-ing

en•ac-tion
en•act-ment
enamel
en•cased
en•chant

en•chant-ing
en•chant-ment
en•cir-cle
en•clave
en•close

en•closed
en•clos-ing
en•clo-sure
en•code
en•coded

en•cod-ing
en•com-pass
en•com-passed
en•com-passes
en•com-pass•ing

en•coun-ter
en•coun-tered
en•coun-ter•ing
en•cour-age
en•cour-aged

en•cour-age-ment
en•cour-ages
en•cour-ag•ing
en•croach
en•croach-ment

en•cum-ber
en•cum-bered
en•cum-brance
en•cum-brances
en•cy-clo-pe•dia

en•cy-clo-pe•dic
end
en•dan-ger
en•dan-gered
en•dan-ger•ing

en•dear-ing
en•dear-ment
en•deavor
en•deav-ored
en•deav-or•ing

en•deav-ors
ended
end•ing
end-less
en•dorse

en•dorsed
en•dorse-ment
en•dorses
en•dors-ing
endow

en•dowed
en•dow-ment
en•dur-able
en•dur-ance
en•dure

en•dur-ing
ene-mies
enemy
en•er-getic
en•er-geti-cally

en•er-gies
en•er-gize
en•er-gized
en•er-giz•ing
en•ergy

en•force
en•force-able
en•forced
en•force-ment
en•forc-ing

en•gage
en•gaged
en•gage-ment
en•gages
en•gag-ing

en•gen-der
en•gen-dered
en•gine
en•gi-neer
en•gi-neered

en•gi-neer•ing
en•grave
en•graved
en•graver
en•grav-ing

en•gross
en•grossed
en•gross-ing
en•gulf
en•hance

en•hanced
en•hance-ment
en•hances
en•hanc-ing
enigma

en•join
en•joined
en•join-ing
enjoy
en•joy-able

en•joyed
en•joy-ing
en•joy-ment
en•large
en•larged

en•large-ment
en•larg-ing
en•lighten
en•light-ened
en•light-en•ing

en•light-en-ment
en•list
en•listed
en•list-ing
en•list-ment

en•liven
en•mity
enor-mity
enor-mous
enor-mously

enough
en•plane
en•rage
en•rich
en•riched

en•rich-ing
en•rich-ment
en•roll
en•rolled
en•rollee

en•roll-ing
en•roll-ment
en route
en•sem-ble
en•shrine

en•shrined
en•sign
en•snare
ensue
en•sued

en•su-ing
en•sure
en•sured
en•sur-ing
en•tail

en•tailed
en•tan-gle
en•tan-gle-ment
enter
en•tered

en•ter-ing
en•ter-prise
en•ter-prises
en•ter-pris•ing
en•ter-tain

en•ter-tained
en•ter-tainer
en•ter-tain•ing
en•ter-tain-ment
en•thuse

en•thused
en•thu-si•asm
en•thu-si•ast
en•thu-si-as•tic
en•thu-si-as-ti-cally

en•tice
en•tice-ment
en•tire
en•tirely
en•tirety

en•ti-ties
en•ti-tle
en•ti-tled
en•ti-tle-ment
en•ti-tling

en•tity
en•to-mo-log-ical
en•to-molo-gist
en•to-mol•ogy
en•tou-rage

en•trance
en•trances
en•trant
en•trap
en•treat

en•trée
en•trench
en•trench-ment
en•tre-pre-neur
en•tre-pre-neur•ial

en•tries
en•trust
en•trusted
en•trust-ing
entry

en•try-gram
entry-way
enu-mer-able
enu-mer•ate
enu-mer-ated

enu-mer-at•ing
enu-mera-tion
enu-mera-tive
enun-ci•ate
enun-cia-tion

en•velop *(v.)*
en•ve-lope *(n.)*
en•vi-able
en•vi-ous
en•vi-ron-ment

en•vi-ron-men•tal
en•vi-ron-men-tally
en•vi-rons
en•vi-sion
en•vi-sioned

envoy
envy
en•zyme
epi-cen•ter
epi-demic

epi-der•mis
epi-gram
epi-lepsy
epi-lep•tic
epi-logue

epi-sode
epis-tle
epi-taph
epit-ome
epoxy

equa-ble
equal
equaled
equal-ity
equal-iza-tion

equal-ize
equal-ized
equal-izes
equal-iz•ing
equally

equate	er•rand	es•tab-lish•ing
equated	er•rant	es•tab-lish-ment
equa-tion	er•ratic	es•tate
equa-tor	er•rati-cally	es•teem
eques-trian	er•ro-ne•ous	es•teemed
equi-lat-eral	er•ro-ne-ously	es•ti-ma•ble
equi-lib-rium	error	es•ti-mate
equine	er•rors	es•ti-mated
equip	eru-dite	es•ti-mat•ing
equip-ment	erupt	es•ti-ma-tion
equipped	erup-tion	es•trange
equip-ping	es•ca-late	es•trange-ment
eq•ui-ta•ble	es•ca-lated	etch-ing
eq•ui-ta•bly	es•ca-lat•ing	eter-nal
eq•ui-ties	es•ca-la-tion	eter-nally
eq•uity	es•ca-la•tor	eter-nity
equiva-lence	es•ca-pade	ethe-real
equiva-len-cies	es•cape	eth-ical
equiva-lency	es•caped	ethi-cally
equiva-lent	es•capee	eth•ics
equivo-cal	es•cheat	eth•nic
era	es•chew	eth-nic•ity
eradi-cate	es•chewed	etio-log-ical
eradi-cat•ing	es•cort	eti-quette
eradi-ca-tion	es•corted	ety-mol•ogy
erase	es•crow	eu•lo-gize
erased	esopha-gus	eu•logy
eraser	es•pe-cial	eu•phe-mism
erases	es•pe-cially	eu•pho-ria
eras-ing	es•pio-nage	eu•reka
era-sure	es•pouse	evacu-ate
ere	esprit de corps	evacu-ated
erect	es•quire	evacu-ation
erected	essay	evade
erect-ing	es•sence	evaded
erec-tion	es•sen-tial	evad-ing
erode	es•sen-tially	evalu-ate
eroded	es•tab-lish	evalu-ated
ero-sion	es•tab-lished	evalu-at•ing
ero-sive	es•tab-lishes	evalu-ation

evalu-ative
evalu-ator
evan-ge-lism
evan-ge-list
evan-ge-lize

evapo-rate
evapo-rated
evapo-ra-tion
evapo-ra-tive
evapo-ra·tor

eva-sion
eva-sive
eve
even
eve-ning

evenly
event
event-ful
even-tual
even-tu-ally

ever
ever-green
ever-lasting
ever-more
every

every-body
every-day
every-one
every-thing
every-where

evict
evic-tion
evi-dence
evi-denced
evi-dences

evi-denc·ing
evi-dent
evi-den-tial
evi-dently
evil

evince
evinced
evo-lu-tion
evo-lu-tion·ary
evo-lu-tion·ist

evolve
evolved
evolv-ing
exact
ex·act-ing

ex·actly
ex·ag-ger·ate
ex·ag-ger-ated
ex·ag-gera-tion
exalt

exam
ex·ami-na-tion
ex·am-ine
ex·am-ined
ex·am-iner

ex·am-in·ing
ex·am-ple
ex·as-per·ate
ex·as-per-ated
ex·as-per-at-edly

ex·as-pera-tion
ex·ca-vate
ex·ca-vated
ex·ca-vat·ing
ex·ca-va-tion

ex·ceed
ex·ceeded
ex·ceed-ing
ex·ceed-ingly
excel

ex·celled
ex·cel-lence
ex·cel-lency
ex·cel-lent
ex·cel-lently

ex·cel-sior
ex·cept
ex·cepted
ex·cept-ing
ex·cep-tion

ex·cep-tional
ex·cep-tion-ally
ex·cerpt
ex·cess
ex·cesses

ex·ces-sive
ex·ces-sively
ex·change
ex·change-able
ex·changed

ex·changes
ex·chang-ing
ex·cise
ex·ci-sion
ex·cit-able

ex·cite
ex·cited
ex·cite-ment
ex·cit-ing
ex·cit-ingly

ex·claim
ex·cla-ma-tion
ex·clama-tory
ex·clude
ex·cluded

ex·clud-ing
ex·clu-sion
ex·clu-sive
ex·clu-sively
ex·clu-sive-ness

ex·clu-siv·ity
ex·cru-ci·ate
ex·cru-ci-at·ing
ex·cur-sion
ex·cus-able

ex•cuse
ex•cused
ex•cuses
ex•cus-ing
exe-cute

exe-cuted
exe-cut•ing
exe-cu-tion
exe-cu-tioner
ex•ecu-tive

ex•ecu-tor
ex•ecu-tory
ex•em-plary
ex•em-pli-fies
ex•em-plify

ex•empt
ex•empted
ex•empt-ing
ex•emp-tion
ex•er-cise

ex•er-cised
ex•er-cises
ex•er-cis•ing
exert
ex•erted

ex•ert-ing
ex•er-tion
ex•hale
ex•haust
ex•hausted

ex•haust-ible
ex•haust-ing
ex•haus-tion
ex•haus-tive
ex•hibit

ex•hib-ited
ex•hib-it•ing
ex•hi-bi-tion
ex•hibi-tor
ex•hila-rate

ex•hila-ra-tion
ex•hort
ex•hor-ta-tion
ex•hume
exile

exist
ex•isted
ex•is-tence
ex•is-tent
ex•ist-ing

ex•ists
exit
ex•it-ing
exo•dus
ex•on-er•ate

ex•or-bi-tant
ex•or-cise
ex•or-cist
ex•otic
ex•pand

ex•pand-able
ex•panded
ex•pand-ing
ex•panse
ex•pan-si•ble

ex•pan-sion
ex•pan-sion•ary
ex•pan-sive
ex parte
ex•pa-ti•ate

ex•pa-tri•ate
ex•pect
ex•pec-tancy
ex•pec-tant
ex•pec-ta-tion

ex•pected
ex•pect-ing
ex•pe-di-ency
ex•pe-di•ent
ex•pe-di-ently

ex•pe-dite
ex•pe-dited
ex•pe-dit•ing
ex•pe-di-tion
ex•pe-di-tious

ex•pe-di-tiously
ex•pe-di•tor
expel
ex•pelled
ex•pend

ex•pend-able
ex•pended
ex•pend-ing
ex•pen-di-ture
ex•pense

ex•pensed
ex•pens-ing
ex•pen-sive
ex•pe-ri-ence
ex•pe-ri-enced

ex•pe-ri-ences
ex•pe•ri-enc•ing
ex•peri-ment
ex•peri-men•tal
ex•peri-men-tally

ex•peri-men-ta-tion
ex•peri-mented
ex•peri-ment•ing
ex•pert
ex•per-tise

ex•pertly
ex•pi-ra-tion
ex•pi-ra-tory
ex•pire
ex•pired

ex•pir-ing
ex•piry
ex•plain
ex•plained
ex•plain-ing

ex·pla-na-tion
ex·plana-tory
ex·plicit
ex·plic-itly
ex·plic-it-ness

ex·plode
ex·ploded
ex·plod-ing
ex·ploit
ex·ploi-ta-tion

ex·ploited
ex·ploit-ing
ex·plo-ra-tion
ex·plor-atory
ex·plore

ex·plored
ex·plorer
ex·plor-ing
ex·plo-sion
ex·plo-sive

ex·po-nent
ex·port
ex·ported
ex·porter
ex·port-ing

ex·pose
ex·posed
ex·pos-ing
ex·po-si-tion
ex·po-sure

ex·pound
ex·press
ex·pressed
ex·presses
ex·press-ing

ex·pres-sion
ex·pres-sive
ex·pressly
express-way
ex·pul-sion

ex·qui-site
ex·qui-sitely
ex·tem-po-ra-ne·ous
ex·tend
ex·tended

ex·tend-able
ex·tend-ing
ex·ten-sion
ex·ten-sive
ex·ten-sively

ex·tent
ex·tenu-ate
ex·tenu-at·ing
ex·te-rior
ex·ter-mi-nate

ex·ter-mi-nated
ex·ter-mi-nat·ing
ex·ter-mi-na-tion
ex·ter-mi-na·tor
ex·ter-nal

ex·ter-nally
ex·tinct
ex·tinc-tion
ex·tin-guish
ex·tin-guished

ex·tin-guisher
ex·tort
ex·tor-tion
extra
ex·tract

ex·tracted
ex·tract-ing
ex·trac-tion
ex·trac-tor
ex·tra-cur-ricu·lar

ex·tra-dite
ex·tra-di-tion
ex·tra-mu·ral
ex·tra-ne·ous
ex·traor-di·narily

ex·traor-di-nary
ex·trapo-late
ex·trapo-lated
ex·trapo-la-tion
ex·trava-gance

ex·trava-gant
ex·trava-ganza
ex·treme
ex·tremely
ex·tremi-ties

ex·trem-ity
ex·trin-sic
ex·trude
ex·tru-sion
exu-ber-ance

exu-ber·ant
exult
ex·ul-tant
ex·ul-ta-tion
eye

eye-brow
eye-glass
eye-glasses
eye·let
eye·lid

eye-sight
eye-sore
eye-witness

_F_____

fable
fa·bled
fab·ric
fab-ri-cate
fab-ri-cated

fab-ri-cat·ing
fab-ri-ca-tion
fab-ri-ca·tor
fabu-lous
fa·cade

F

face
faced
faces
facet
fac•ets

fa•cial
fac•ile
fa•cili-tate
fa•cili-tated
fa•cili-tat•ing

fa•cili-ta•tor
fa•cili-ties
fa•cil-ity
fac•ing
fac-sim•ile

fact
fac-tion
fac•tor
fac-tored
fac-to-rial

fac-to-ries
fac-tory
fac-tual
fac-ul-ta-tive
fac-ul-ties

fac-ulty
fade
faded
fad•ing
Fahr-en-heit

fail
failed
fail-ing
fail-ure
faint

faint-ing
fair
fairer
fair-grounds
fairly

fair--minded
fair-ness
fair-way
faith
faith-ful

faith-fully
faith-ful-ness
fal•con
fall
fal-la-cies

fal-la-cious
fal-lacy
fallen
fal-li•ble
fall-ing

fall-out
false
false-hood
falsely
fal-si-fi-ca-tion

fal-si-fied
fal-sify
fal-si-fy•ing
fal-ter
fame

fa•mil-iar
fa•mil-iar•ity
fa•mil-iar-iza-tion
fa•mil-iar•ize
fa•mil-iar-iz•ing

fami-lies
fam•ily
fam•ine
fam•ish
fa•mous

fan
fa•natic
fa•nat-ical
fan-cied
fan-cies

fan-ci•ful
fancy
fan-fare
fan-ta-sies
fan-tas•tic

fan-tasy
far
farce
fare
fare-well

far-fetched
farm
farmed
farmer
farm-ers

farm-ing
farm owner
farm worker
far-sighted
far-ther

far-thest
fas-ci-nate
fas-ci-nated
fas-ci-nat•ing
fas-ci-nat-ingly

fas-ci-na-tion
fash-ion
fash-ion-able
fash-ioned
fast

fas•ten
fas-tened
fas-tener
fas-ten•ing
faster

fast-est
fat
fatal
fa•tal-is•tic
fa•tali-ties

fa•tal-ity
fate
fate-ful
fa•ther
fathom

fa•tigue
fa•tigu-ing
fat•ten
fau•cet
fault

faulted
fault-finder
fault-ing
fault-less
faulty

favor
fa•vor-able
fa•vor-ably
fa•vor-ing
fa•vor-ite

fa•vor-it•ism
faze
fear
feared
fear-ful

fear-ing
fear-less
fea-si-bil•ity
fea-si•ble
feast

feat
feather
feather-weight
fea-ture
fea-tured

fea-tur•ing
Feb-ru•ary
fed
fed-eral
fed-er-al•ist

fed-er-ally
fed-er•ate
fed-er-ated
fed-era-tion
fee

fee•ble
feed
feed-back
feeder
feed-ing

feel
feel-ing
feet
feign
fe•lici-ta-tion

fe•lici-tous
fe•lic-ity
fe•line
fell
fel•low

fel-low-ship
felo-nies
fel•ony
felt
fe•male

femi-nine
femi-nin•ity
fence
fenced
fences

fenc-ing
fender
fer-ment
fer-mented
fer-men-ta-tion

fe•ro-cious
fer•ret
fer-ret•ing
fer-rous
fer-rule

fer-tile
fer-til•ity
fer-til-iza-tion
fer-til•ize
fer-til-izer

fer-til-iz•ers
fer-vent
fer•vor
fes-ti•val
fes-tive

fes-tivi-ties
fes-tiv•ity
fetal
fe•tish
fetus

fe•tuses
feud
feu•dal
fever
few

fewer
few•est
fi•ancé
fi•asco
fiber

fiber-board
fiber-glass
fickle
fic-tion
fic-tional

fic-tion-al•ize
fic-ti-tious
fi•del-ity
fi•du-ciary
field

fielded
fielder
field-ing
fierce
fiercely

fiery
fi·esta
fif-teen
fif-teenth
fifth

fif-ti·eth
fifty
fight
fighter
fight-ing

fig-ment
figs
figu-ra-tive
fig·ure
fig-ured

figu-rine
fig-ur·ing
fila-ment
file
filed

filer
filet
fili-bus·ter
fil·ing
fill

filled
filler
fill-ers
fill-ing
film

filmed
film-ing
film-strip
fil·ter
filth

filthy
final
fi·nale
fi·nal-ist
fi·nal-ity

fi·nal-iza-tion
fi·nal-ize
fi·nal-ized
fi·nal-iz·ing
fi·nally

fi·nance
fi·nanced
fi·nances
fi·nan-cial
fi·nan-cially

fi·nan-cier
fi·nanc-ing
find
finder
find-ing

fine
fined
finer
fin·ery
fin·est

fi·nesse
fine-tuning
fin·ger
fin-ger·ing
finger-print

finger-tip
finis
fin·ish
fin-ished
fin-isher

fin-ishes
fin-ish·ing
fi·nite
fir
fire

fire-arm
fire-cracker
fired
fire-place
fire-places

fire-proof
fire-proofing
fire-side
fire-works
fir·ing

firm
fir-ma-ment
firmed
firmer
firm-ing

firmly
firm-ness
first
first-hand
firstly

fis·cal
fish
fish-er·ies
fish-ery
fishes

fish-ing
fis-sion
fis-sure
fisti-cuffs
fis-tula

fit
fit-ness
fit·ted
fit-ting
five

five-fold
fix
fixa-tion
fixed
fixer

fixes
fix·ing
fix-ture
fiz·zle
flac-cid

flag
fla-grant
fla-grantly
flair
flake

flak-ing
flam-boy-ance
flam-boy•ant
flame
flam-ing

fla-mingo
flam-ma-bil•ity
flam-ma•ble
flange
flanges

flange-way
flan-nel
flare
flared
flar-ing

flash
flasher
flashes
flash-ing
flash-light

flashy
flat
flatly
flat-ness
flat-ter

flat-tered
flat-tery
flat-ware
fla•vor
fla-vor•ful

flaw
flaw-less
flea
fledge
fledg-ing

fledg-ling
flee
flee-ing
fleet
fleet-ing

flesh
fleshy
flew
flex
flexi-bil•ity

flex-ible
flex-ing
flex-ural
flicker
flier

fli•ers
flies
flight
flimsy
flip

flip-pant
flip-ping
flir-ta-tion
float
floa-ta-tion

floated
floater
float-ing
flock
flood

flooded
flood-ing
flood-light
flood-plain
flood-water

floor
floored
floor-ing
flop-pi-ness
floppy

flora
flo•ral
flo-res-cence
flo-res-cent
Flor-ida

flo-rist
flo-ta-tion
floun-der
flour
flour-ish

flow
flow-age
flower
flow-ers
flow-ing

fluc-tu•ate
fluc-tu-ated
fluc-tu-at•ing
fluc-tua-tion
flu-ency

flu•ent
flu-ently
fluid
flu•ids
fluo-res-cence

fluo-res-cent
fluo-ri-date
fluo-ride
flur-ries
flurry

flush
flushed
flushes
flush-ing
flut-ter

fly
flyer
fly•ers
fly•ing
fly-leaf

fly-paper
foam
foamed
foam-ing
focal

focus
fo·cused
fo·cuses
fo·cus-ing
fogged

fog-horn
foil
foist
fold
folded

folder
fold-ers
fold-ing
fold-out
fo·liage

folio
folk-lore
folks
fol-li·cle
fol-lies

fol·low
fol-lowed
fol-lower
fol-low·ers
fol-low·ing

follow--up
folly
fond
fon-dant
fondly

fond-ness
fon·due
food
food-stuff
fool-ish

fool-proof
foot
foot-age
foot-ball
foot-hill

foot-hold
foot-ing
foot-note
foot-print
foot-rest

foot-steps
foot-stool
foot-wear
for
for-bear-ance

for·bid
for-bid·den
for-bid-ding
force
forced

force-ful
for-ceps
forces
forc-ible
forc-ibly

forc-ing
fore-arm
fore-armed
fore-cast
fore-casted

fore-caster
fore-cast·ing
fore-close
fore-closed
fore-clo-sure

fore-front
forego
fore-go·ing
fore-gone
fore-ground

fore-hand
fore-head
for-eign
for-eigner
fore-most

fore-noon
fo·ren-sic
fore-run·ner
fore-see
fore-see-able

fore-seen
fore-sight
fore-sighted
for·est
fore-stall

for-ester
for-estry
fore-tell
fore-told
for-ever

fore-warn
fore-warn·ing
fore-word
for-feit
for-feited

for-feit·ing
for-fei-ture
forge
forged
forger

forg-er·ies
forg-ery
for·get
for-get·ful
for-get-ting

forg-ing
for-give
for-give-ness
for·got
for-got·ten

ork	for-tu-nate	frag-ment
ork-truck	for-tu-nately	frag-men-ta-tion
or-lorn	for-tune	frag-mented
orm	forty	fra-grance
or·mal	forum	fra-grant
or-mali-ties	fo·rums	frail
or-mal·ity	for-ward	frame
or-mal·ize	for-warded	framed
or-mal-ized	for-ward·ing	frame-work
or-mally	fos·sil	fram-ing
or·mat	fos·ter	fran-chise
or-ma-tion	fos-tered	fran-chised
or-ma-tive	fos-ter·ing	fran-chi·see
or-mat-ting	fought	fran-chises
ormed	foul	fran-chis·ing
or·mer *(adj.)*	fouled	fran-chi·sor
ormer *(n.)*	foul-ing	frank
or-merly	found	frank-furter
or-mica	foun-da-tion	frankly
or-mi-da·ble	founded	frank-ness
orm-ing	founder	fran-tic
or-mula	found-ers	fran-ti-cally
or-mu·las	found-ing	fra-ter·nal
or-mu-late	found-ries	fra-ter-nity
or-mu-lated	foundry	fraud
or-mu-lat·ing	foun-tain	fraudu-lent
or-mu-la·tion	four	free
or-sake	four--fifths	freed
or-saken	four-fold	free-dom
orth	four-some	free-ing
orth-com·ing	four-teen	freely
orth-right	fourth	free-standing
orth-with	foyer	free-way
or-ti·eth	frac-tion	freeze
or-ti-fi-ca-tion	frac-tional	freezer
or-ti-fied	frac-ture	freezes
or-ti-fies	frac-tured	freez-ing
or-tify	frac-tur·ing	freight
or-ti-tude	frag-ile	freighter
or-tu-itous	fra-gil·ity	freight-ing

frenzy
fre-quen-cies
fre-quency
fre-quent
fre-quently

fresh
freshen
fresh-ness
fric-tion
Fri·day

friend
friend-less
friend-li-ness
friendly
friend-ship

frieze
frighten
fright-ened
fright-en·ing
fright-ful

frigid
fringe
fringes
fri-vol·ity
frivo-lous

frog
from
front
front-age
fron-tal

fron-tier
front-ing
fron-tis-piece
frost
frost-bite

frosted
frost-ing
frost-less
frosty
frown

frowned
fro·zen
fruc-tose
fru·gal
fru-gal·ity

fruit
fruit-ful
fru-ition
fruit-less
frus-trate

frus-trated
frus-trat·ing
frus-tra-tion
fry·ing
fuel

fueled
fu·el-ing
fu·gi-tive
ful-fill
ful-filled

ful-fill·ing
ful-fill-ment
full
fuller
full-est

full--time *(adj.)*
fully
ful-mi-nate
fum·ble
fumes

fu·mi-gate
fun
func-tion
func-tional
func-tioned

func-tion·ing
fund
fun-da-men·tal
fun-da-men-tally
funded

funder
fund-ing
fu·neral
fun-gi-cide
fun·gus

fun·nel
fun-neled
fun-nier
fun-ni·est
funny

fur-bearer
fur-bish
fu·ri-ous
fur-lough
fur-nace

fur-naces
fur-nish
fur-nished
fur-nishes
fur-nish-ings

fur-ni-ture
fur-rier
fur·row
fur-ther
fur-ther-ance

fur-ther·ing
fur-ther-more
fur-ther-most
fur-thest
fuse

fused
fu·se-lage
fuses
fu·sion
fu·tile

fu·til-ity
fu·ture
fu·tur-ist
fu·tur-is·tic

G _____

gab-ar-dine
ga•bion
gad•get
gai•ety
gain

gained
gain-fully
gain-ing
gala
gal•axy

gal-lant
gal-lantry
gall-bladder
gal-ler•ies
gal-lery

gal•ley
gal•lon
gall-stone
ga•lore
gal-va-nize

gal-va-nized
gal-va-niz•ing
gam•ble
gam-bler
gam-bling

game
gamma
gang
gang-ster
gang-way

gap
ga•rage
ga•rages
gar-bage
gar•den

gar-dener
gar-den•ing
gar•lic
gar-ment
gar•ner

gar-nish
gar-nish-ment
gas
gas-eous
gases

gas•ket
gaso-line
gas-tric
gate
gate-way

gather
gath-ered
gath-er•ing
gauge
gauged

gauges
gaug-ing
gauze
gave
gavel

ga•zebo
ga•zette
gaz•ing
gear
geared

gear-ing
gel
gela-tin
gelled
gem

gen•der
ge•nea-log-ical
ge•ne-alo-gist
ge•ne-al•ogy
gen-eral

gen-er-al•ist
gen-er-ali-ties
gen-er-al•ity
gen-er-al-iza-tion
gen-er-al•ize

gen-er-al-ized
gen-er-ally
gen-er•ate
gen-er-ated
gen-er-at•ing

gen-era-tion
gen-era•tor
ge•neric
gen-er-os•ity
gen-er•ous

gen-er-ously
ge•netic
ge•nial
ge•nius
ge•niuses

gen-teel
gen-tile
gen•tle
gently
genu-ine

genu-inely
geo-graphic
geo-graph-ical
geo-graphi-cally
ge•og-ra•phy

geo-logic
geo-log-ical
ge•olo-gist
geo-met•ric
ge•ome-try

geo-phys-ical
geo-phys•ics
Geor-gia
geo-ther•mal
ge•ra-nium

G

ge•ri•at•ric
ger-mane
ger-mi-nate
ger-mi-nat•ing
ger-on-tol•ogy

ger•und
ges-ture
ges-tur•ing
get
get-away

get-ting
get--together (n.)
gey•ser
ghastly
ghetto

ghost
ghostly
ghost-writer
giant
gift

gifted
gi•gan-tic
gin•ger
ging-ham
gi•raffe

girder
gird-ing
gir•dle
girl
gist

give
give-away (n.)
given
gives
giv•ing

gla-cial
gla-cier
glad
glad-den
gladi-ator

gladly
glam-or•ize
glam-or-ized
glam-or•ous
glam-our

glance
glanc-ing
gland
glan-du•lar
glare

glare-proof
glar-ing
glass
glasses
glass-ful

glass-ware
glau-coma
glaze
glazed
glaz-ing

gleam
gleam-ing
gleaned
glide
glider

glid-ing
glim-mer
glimpse
glimpses
glis-ten

glis-ten•ing
glit-ter
global
globe
gloomy

glo-rify
glo-ri•ous
glory
glos-sary
glossy

glove
glow
glow-ing
glu-cose
glue

glued
glu•ing
gnarled
gnaw-ing
go

goal
go--between (n.)
god
god-send
goer

going
goi•ter
gold
golden
golf

golf-ing
gon-dola
gone
good
good-bye

good-ies
goodly
good-ness
good-will
goofed

goose
goose-neck
gor-geous
gos•pel
gos•sip

got
got•ten
gour-met
gov•ern
gov•er-nance

gov-erned
gov-ern•ing
gov-ern-ment
gov-ern-men•tal
gov-ern-men-tally

gov-er•nor
grab
grab-bing
grace
graced

grace-ful
graces
grac-ing
gra-cious
gra-ciously

gra-cious-ness
gra-da-tion
grade
graded
grader

gra-di•ent
grad-ing
grad-ual
gradu-ally
gradu-ate

gradu-ated
gradu-at•ing
gradu-ation
graf-fito
grain

gram-mar
gram-mar•ian
gram-mat-ical
gra-nary
grand

grand-child
grand-chil-dren
gran-deur
grand-fa-ther
gran-di•ose

grand-mother
grand-par-ents
grand-stand
grange
gran-ite

grant
granted
grantee
grant-ing
grantor

granu-lar
granu-late
granu-lated
granu-la-tion
gran-ule

grape
grape-fruit
grape-vine
graph
graphic

graph-ical
graphi-cally
graph-ite
grap-ple
grap-pling

grasp
grasped
grasp-ing
grass
grassed

grasses
grass-hopper
grass--roots *(adj.)*
grate-ful
grate-fully

grate-ful-ness
grati-fi-ca-tion
grati-fied
grati-fy•ing
gra•tis

grati-tude
gra-tu-ities
gra-tu-itous
gra-tu•ity
grave

gravel
grav-eled
gravely
grave-side
grav-est

grave-stone
gravi-tate
gravi-ta-tion
grav-ity
gravy

gray
gray-ish
graz-ing
grease
greases

greasy
great
greater
great-est
greatly

great-ness
greedy
green
green-ery
green-house

green-ish
greet
greeted
greet-ing
gre-gari•ous

grem-lin
gre-nade
grew
grey-hound
grid

griev-ance
griev-ances
griev-ant
grieve
grieved

griev-ous
grill
grille
gri-mace
grind

grinder
grind-ing
grind-stone
grip
grip-per

grip-ping
grit-ting
gro•cer
gro-cer•ies
gro-cery

groggy
groin
groom
groomed
groom-ing

groove
gross
grossed
grossly
gro-tesque

grotto
ground
grounded
ground-ing
ground-less

ground-work
group
grouped
group-ing
grout

grouted
grout-ing
grove
grovel
grow

grower
grow-ers
grow-ing
grown
growth

grudge
grue-some
grum-ble
guar-an•tee
guar-an-teed

guar-an-tee•ing
guar-an•tor
guar-anty
guard
guarded

guard-ian
guard-ian-ship
guard-ing
gu•ber-na-to-rial
guer-rilla

guess
guessed
guesses
guess-ing
guess-work

guest
guid-ance
guide
guided
guide-lines

guide-post
guid-ing
guilt
guilt-less
guilty

guise
gui•tar
gull-ibil•ity
gull-ible
gum

gummed
gun
gunned
gunny-sack
gun-wale

gus•set
gut
gut•ter
gut-ting
gut-tural

guz•zle
gym
gym-na-sium
gym-nast
gym-nas•tic

gy•ne-co-logic
gy•ne-colo-gist
gy•ne-col•ogy
gyp•sum
gypsy

gy•rate
gy•rat-ing
gy•ra-tion

_H_____

habit
habi-tat
habi-ta-tion
hab•its
ha•bit-ual

ha•bitu-ally
had
had-dock
hadn't
hail

hailed
hair
hairdo
hair-line
hairy

half
half-back
half-hearted
half-tone
half-way

hali-but
hall
hal-le-lu·jah
hall-mark
hal-lu-ci-nate

hal-lu-ci-na-tion
hal-lu-ci-no-genic
hall-way
halo
halt

halted
halves
ham-burger
ham·mer
ham-mer·ing

ham-mock
ham·per
ham-pered
ham-per·ing
hand

hand-bag
hand-book
hand-cuff
handed
hand-ful

handi-cap
handi-capped
handi-craft
hand-ily
handi-work

hand-ker-chief
han·dle
handle-bar
han-dled
han-dler

han-dling
hand-made
hand-out (n.)
hand-picked
hand-rail

hand-shake
hand-some
hand-somely
hand-write
hand-writing

hand-written
handy
hang
han·gar
hang-ers

hang-ing
hang--up (n.)
hap-haz·ard
hap·pen
hap-pened

hap-pen·ing
hap-pen-stance
hap-pier
hap-pi·est
hap-pily

hap-pi-ness
happy
ha·rass
ha·rassed
ha·rass-ing

ha·rass-ment
har-bin·ger
har·bor
hard
hard-back

harden
hard-ened
hard-en·ing
harder
hard-est

hard-hearted
hardly
hard-ness
hard-ship
hard-ware

hard-wood
harm
harm-ful
harm-ing
harm-less

har-monic
har-mon·ica
har-mo-ni·ous
har-mo-ni-ously
har-mo-nize

har-mo-niz·ing
har-mony
har-ness
harsh
har-vest

har-vested
har-vester
har-vest·ing
has
hasn't

has·sle
haste
has·ten
has-tened
has-ten·ing

hast-ily
hasty
hatch
hatch-ery
hatch-ing

hate
hate-ful
ha•tred
haughty
haul

haul-age
hauled
haul-ing
haunt
haunted

have
haven
haven't
hav•ing
havoc

Ha•waii
hay
hay-field
hay-stack
hay-wire

haz•ard
haz-ard•ous
haz-ards
hazy
he

head
head-ache
head-board
headed
header

head-ing
head-light
head-line
head-master
head--on

head-phone
head-quar-tered
head-quarters
head-rest
head-room

head-set
head-way
heal
healed
heal-ing

health
health-ful
health-ful-ness
health-ier
healthy

hear
heard
hear-ing
hear-say
heart

heart-ache
heart-breaking
heart-broken
heart-burn
heart-ened

heart-felt
hearth
hearti-est
heart-ily
heart-warming

hearty
heat
heated
heater
hea-then

heather
heat-ing
heaven
heav-enly
heavier

heavily
heavy
heavy--duty
heavy-weight
hec•tic

hedge
heed
heeded
heels
heifer

height
heighten
height-ened
hei-nous
heir

heir-loom
held
he•lia-cally
he•li-cop•ter
he•lium

he'll
hello
hel•met
help
helped

helper
help-ers
help-ful
help-fully
help-ful-ness

help-ing
help-less
help-lessly
he•ma-tol•ogy
hemi-sphere

hemmed
he•mo-di-aly•sis
hem-or-rhage
hem-or-rhag•ing
hem-or-rhoids

he•mo-static
hence
hence-forth
he•patic
hepa-ti•tis

her	hi·ber-nate	his-toric
her·ald	hi·bis-cus	his-tor-ical
herb	hic·cup	his-tori-cally
her-bi-cide	hick-ory	his-to-ries
herd	hid·den	his-tory
here	hide	hit
here-abouts	hid-eous	hitch-hike
here-above	hid·ing	hith-er-most
here-after	hi·er-ar·chy	hith-erto
hereby	high	hit-ting
he·redi-tary	higher	hoard-ing
he·red-ity	high-est	hob-bies
herein	high-land	hob·ble
here-in-above	high-light	hobby
here-in-after	high-lighted	hob-by·ist
hereof	high-lighting	hockey
hereon	highly	hoist
her·esy	high-way	hold
here-tic	hik·ing	holder
hereto	hi·lari-ous	hold-ers
here-to-fore	hill	hold-ing
here-under	hill-billy	hold-out
here-with	him	hold-over
heri-tage	him-self	hole
her·nia	hin·der	holi-day
her-ni-ated	hin-dered	ho·li-ness
hero	hin-drance	hol·low
he·roes	hind-sight	holly
he·roic	hinge	ho·lo-caust
her-self	hinges	ho·lo-graph
hesi-tancy	hint	hol-stein
hesi-tant	hinted	hol-ster
hesi-tate	hip-po-pota·mus	holy
hesi-tated	hire	hom·age
hesi-ta-tion	hired	home
het-ero-ge-ne·ity	hir·ing	home-coming
het-ero-ge-neous	his	home-land
hexa-gon	His-panic	home-less
hex-ago·nal	his-ta-mine	home-like
hia·tus	his-to-rian	homely

home-made
home-maker
home-making
home-owner
home-room

home-sick
home-spun
home-stead
home-work
ho•mi-cide

ho•mo-ge-neous
ho•moge-nize
ho•moge-nized
ho•molo-gous
hom-onym

honed
hon•est
hon-estly
hon-esty
honey

honey-moon
hon•ing
honk-ing
honor
hon-or-able

hon-or-ably
hono-rar•ium
hon-or•ary
hon-ored
hon-or•ing

hon•ors
hood-lum
hook
hooked
hookup

hoop
hope
hoped
hope-ful
hope-fully

hope-less
hope-lessly
hope-less-ness
hop•ing
hop•per

hop-ping
ho•ri-zon
hori-zon•tal
hori-zon-tally
hor-mone

horn
horo-scope
hor-ren-dous
hor-ri•ble
hor•rid

hor-rify
hor•ror
horse
horse-back
horse-play

horse-power
horse-shoe
hor-ta-tory
hor-ti-cul-tural
hor-ti-cul-ture

hor-ti-cul-tur•ist
hose
hoses
ho•siery
hos-pice

hos-pi-ta•ble
hos-pi•tal
hos-pi-tal•ity
hos-pi-tal-iza-tion
hos-pi-tal-ized

host
hos-tage
hosted
host-ess
host-esses

hos-tile
host-ing
hot
hotel
hot-line

hot•ter
hot-test
hour
hourly
house

house-broken
house-cleaning
housed
house-hold
house-keeper

house-keeping
house-parents
houses
house-warming
house-work

hous-ing
hover
hov-er•ing
how
how-ever

hub
hub•bub
hub•cap
hud•dle
huge

hull
human
hu•mane
hu•man-is•tic
hu•mani-tar•ian

hu•mani-ties
hu•man-ity
hu•man-ize
hu•manly
hum•ble

humid
hu·midi-fi-ca-tion
hu·midi-fier
hu·mid-ity
hu·mili-ate

hu·mili-ation
hu·mil-ity
humor
hu·mor-ist
hu·mor-ous

hump-back
hunch
hunches
hun-dred
hun-dredth

hundred-weight
hung
hun·ger
hun·ger·ing
hun·gry

hunt
hunter
hunt-ing
hur·dle
hur·rah

hur-ri-cane
hur-ried
hur-riedly
hurry
hurt

hurt-ful
hus-band
hus-bandry
husky
hus·tle

hy·brid
hy·drant
hy·drau-lic
hy·dro-car·bon
hy·dro-elec-tric

hy·dro-elec-tri·cal
hy·dro-gen
hy·dro-plane
hy·dro-static
hy·drox-ide

hy·giene
hy·gienic
hy·gien-ist
hymn
hy·per-ac-tive

hy·per-ac-tiv·ity
hy·per-crit-ical
hy·per-ten-sion
hy·phen
hy·phen-ate

hyp-no·sis
hyp-notic
hyp-no-tist
hyp-no-tize
hy·po-ac-tiv·ity

hy·poc-risy
hypo-crite
hypo-crit-ical
hy·po-der·mic
hy·pothe-sis

hy·pothe-size
hy·po-thet-ical
hys-te·ria
hys-ter-ical
hys-ter·ics

___I___

I
ice
iced
ici·cle
icing

I'd
Idaho
idea
ideal
ide-al·ism

ide-al·ist
ide-ally
iden-ti·cal
iden-ti-cally
iden-ti-fi-able

iden-ti-fi-ca-tion
iden-ti-fied
iden-ti-fier
iden-ti-fies
iden-tify

iden-ti-fy·ing
iden-tity
ideo-log-ical
ide-ol·ogy
idiom

idle
idle-ness
idol
idola-try
idol-ize

if
ig·nite
ig·nited
ig·ni-tion
ig·no-rance

ig·no-rant
ig·nore
ig·nored
ig·nor-ing
I'll

ill
il·le-gal
il·le-gally
il·leg-ible
il·le-giti-macy

I

il·le·giti·mate
il·licit
Il·li·nois
il·lit-er·acy
il·lit-er·ate

ill-ness
ill-nesses
il·log-ical
il·lu-mi-nate
il·lu-mi-nated

il·lu-mi-nat·ing
il·lu-mi-na-tion
il·lu-sion
il·lus-trate
il·lus-trated

il·lus-trat·ing
il·lus-tra-tion
il·lus-tra-tive
il·lus-tra·tor
il·lus-tri·ous

I'm
image
im·ag-ery
images
imag-in-able

imagi-nary
imagi-na-tion
imagi-na-tive
imagi-na-tively
imag-ine

imag-ined
imag-in·ing
im·bal-ance
im·bal-ances
im·be-cile

im·bibe
imi-tate
imi-ta-tion
imi-ta·tor
im·macu-late

im·ma-te-rial
im·ma-ture
im·ma-tu-rity
im·mea-sur-able
im·mea-sur-ably

im·me-di·ate
im·me-di-ately
im·mense
im·mensely
im·merse

im·mer-sion
im·mi-grant
im·mi-gra-tion
im·mi-nence
im·mi-nent

im·mo-bile
im·mod-est
im·moral
im·mo-ral·ity
im·mor-tal

im·mor-tal·ity
im·mov-able
im·mune
im·mu-nity
im·mu-nize

im·mu-ni-za-tion
im·mu-nized
im·pact
im·pacted
im·pact-ing

im·pair
im·paired
im·pair-ing
im·pair-ment
im·panel

im·part
im·parted
im·par-tial
im·par-tial·ity
im·par-tially

im·pass-able
im·passe
im·pas-sive
im·pa-tient
im·peach

im·pec-ca·ble
im·ped-ance
im·pedi-ment
impel
im·pelled

im·pend-ing
im·pene-tra·ble
im·pera-tive
im·per-fect
im·per-fec-tion

im·pe-rial
im·peril
im·per-mis-si·ble
im·per-sonal
im·per-son·ate

im·per-son-ator
im·per-ti-nence
im·per-ti-nent
im·petu-ous
im·pe-tus

im·pinge
im·pinge-ment
im·ping-ing
im·plau-si·ble
im·ple-ment

im·ple-men-ta-tion
im·ple-mented
im·ple-ment·ing
im·pli-cate
im·pli-ca-tion

im·plicit
im·plic-itly
im·plied
im·plies
im·plore

imply
im•po-lite
im•port
im•por-tance
im•por-tant

im•por-tantly
im•por-ta-tion
im•ported
im•porter
im•port-ing

im•por-tune
im•por-tun•ing
im•pose
im•posed
im•poses

im•pos-ing
im•po-si-tion
im•pos-si-bil•ity
im•pos-si•ble
im•pos-tor

im•po-tency
im•pound
im•pounded
im•pound-ment
im•pov-er-ished

im•prac-ti-ca•ble
im•prac-ti•cal
im•prac-ti-cal•ity
im•preg-na-tion
im•press

im•pressed
im•presses
im•press-ible
im•press-ing
im•pres-sion

im•pres-sion-able
im•pres-sive
im•print
im•printed
im•print-ing

im•prison
im•pris-oned
im•pris-on-ment
im•prob-able
im•promptu

im•proper
im•prop-erly
im•pro-pri•ety
im•prove
im•proved

im•prove-ment
im•prov-ing
im•pro-vi-sa-tion
im•pro-vise
im•pru-dence

im•pru-dent
im•pulse
im•pulses
im•pul-sive
im•pul-sive-ness

im•pu-nity
im•pure
im•pu-rity
in
in•abil-ity

in ab-sen•tia
in•ac-ces-si•ble
in•ac-cu-ra-cies
in•ac-cu-racy
in•ac-cu-rate

in•ac-tion
in•ac-tive
in•ac-tiv•ity
in•ade-qua-cies
in•ade-quacy

in•ade-quate
in•ade-quately
in•ad-mis-si•ble
in•ad-ver-tence
in•ad-ver-tent

in•ad-ver-tently
in•ad-vis-able
in•alien-able
in•ani-mate
in•ap-pro-pri•ate

in•ap-pro-pri-ately
in•ap-ti-tude
in•ar-ticu-late
in•as-much
in•au-di•ble

in•au-gu•ral
in•au-gu-rate
in•au-gu-rated
in•au-gu-ra-tion
in•aus-pi-cious

in•bred
in•can-des-cence
in•can-des-cent
in•ca-pa•ble
in•ca-paci-tate

in•ca-pac•ity
in•car-cer•ate
in•cense
in•cen-tive
in•cep-tion

in•ces-sant
inch
inches
inch-ing
in•ci-dence

in•ci-dences
in•ci-dent
in•ci-den•tal
in•ci-den-tally
in•cin-er•ate

in•cin-era-tion
in•cin-era•tor
in•ci-sion
in•ci-sive
in•cite

in·clem·ent
in·cli·na·tion
in·cline
in·clined
in·clud·able

in·clude
in·cluded
in·clud·ing
in·clu·sion
in·clu·sive

in·cog·nito
in·co·her·ence
in·co·her·ent
in·come
in·com·ing

in·com·pa·ra·ble
in·com·pat·ible
in·com·pe·tence
in·com·pe·tency
in·com·pe·tent

in·com·plete
in·com·pre·hen·si·ble
in·com·pre·hen·sion
in·con·ceiv·able
in·con·clu·sive

in·con·gru·ence
in·con·gru·ent
in·con·se·quent
in·con·se·quen·tial
in·con·sid·er·ate

in·con·sis·ten·cies
in·con·sis·tency
in·con·sis·tent
in·con·spicu·ous
in·con·test·abil·ity

in·con·ve·nience
in·con·ve·nienced
in·con·ve·niences
in·con·ve·nienc·ing
in·con·ve·nient

in·con·vert·ible
in·cor·po·rate
in·cor·po·rated
in·cor·po·rat·ing
in·cor·po·ra·tion

in·cor·rect
in·cor·rectly
in·cor·ri·gi·ble
in·crease
in·creased

in·creases
in·creas·ing
in·creas·ingly
in·cred·ible
in·cred·ibly

in·cre·ment
in·cre·men·tal
in·crimi·nate
in·cu·bate
in·cu·ba·tor

in·cum·bency
in·cum·bent
incur
in·cur·able
in·curred

in·cur·rence
in·cur·ring
in·debted
in·debt·ed·ness
in·de·cent

in·de·ci·sion
in·de·co·rum
in·deed
in·de·fen·si·ble
in·defi·nite

in·defi·nitely
in·del·ible
in·dem·ni·fi·ca·tion
in·dem·ni·fied
in·dem·nify

in·dem·nity
in·dent
in·den·ta·tion
in·dented
in·den·tion

in·den·ture
in·de·pen·dence
in·de·pen·dent
in·de·pen·dently
in·de·scrib·able

in·de·struc·ti·ble
in·de·ter·mi·nate
index
in·dexed
in·dexes

in·dex·ing
in·di·cate
in·di·cated
in·di·cat·ing
in·di·ca·tion

in·dica·tive
in·di·ca·tor
in·di·ces
in·dict
in·dict·ment

in·dif·fer·ence
in·dif·fer·ent
in·dige·nous
in·di·gent
in·di·gest·ible

in·di·ges·tion
in·dig·nant
in·dig·na·tion
in·dig·ni·ties
in·dig·nity

in·di·rect
in·di·rectly
in·dis·creet
in·dis·cre·tion
in·dis·crimi·nate

in·dis-crimi-nately
in·dis-pens-able
in·dis-posed
in·dis-tinct
in·di-vid·ual

in·di-vidu-al·ist
in·di-vidu-al·ity
in·di-vidu-al-iza-tion
in·di-vidu-al·ize
in·di-vidu-al-ized

in·di-vidu-al-iz·ing
in·di-vidu-ally
in·di-vis-ible
in·doc-tri-nate
in·doc-tri-nat·ing

in·do-lence
in·do-lent
in·door
in·duce
in·duced

in·duce-ment
in·duct
in·duc-tion
in·dulge
in·dul-gence

in·dulg-ing
in·dus-trial
in·dus-tri-al·ist
in·dus-tri-al-iza-tion
in·dus-tri-al-ized

in·dus-tri-ally
in·dus-tries
in·dus-tri·ous
in·dus-try
in·ed-ible

in·ef-fec-tive
in·ef-fi-cien-cies
in·ef-fi-ciency
in·ef-fi-cient
in·eli-gi·ble

inept
in·equali-ties
in·equal-ity
in·eq-ui-ta·ble
in·eq-ui-ties

in·eq-uity
in·er-tia
in·es-cap-able
in·evi-ta·ble
in·ex-act

in·ex-cus-able
in·ex-haust-ible
in·exo-ra·ble
in·ex-pen-sive
in·ex-pe-ri-enced

in·ex-plain-able
in·fal-li·ble
in·fa-mous
in·fancy
in·fant

in·fan-tile
in·fan-try
in·fatu-ation
in·fect
in·fected

in·fec-tion
infer
in·fer-ence
in·fer-ences
in·fe-rior

in·fe-ri-or·ity
in·ferred
in·fest
in·fes-ta-tion
in·fested

in·fest-ing
in·fi-del·ity
in·fil-trate
in·fil-tra-tion
in·fi-nite

in·fini-tesi·mal
in·fini-tive
in·fin-ity
in·firm
in·fir-mary

in·fir-mity
in·flam-ma·ble
in·flam-ma-tion
in·flate
in·flated

in·fla-tion
in·fla-tion·ary
in·flec-tion
in·flex-ible
in·flict

in·flic-tion
in·flu-ence
in·flu-enced
in·flu-ences
in·flu-en-tial

in·flu-enza
in·flux
in·form
in·for-mal
in·for-mal·ity

in·for-mally
in·for-mant
in·for-ma-tion
in·for-ma-tional
in·for-ma-tive

in·formed
in·former
in·form-ing
in·frac-tion
infra-red

infra-struc-ture
in·fre-quent
in·fre-quently
in·fringe
in·fringe-ment

in·fu-ri·ate
in·fused
in·fu-sion
in·ge-nious
in·ge-nu·ity

in·ges-tion
in·grained
in·grati-tude
in·gre-di·ent
in·gress

in·habit
in·hab-it·ant
in·ha-la-tion
in·hale
in·haler

in·her-ent
in·her-ently
in·herit
in·heri-tance
in·her-ited

in·hibit
in·hib-it·ing
in·hi-bi-tion
in·hibi-tor
in·hibi-tory

in·hos-pi-ta·ble
in·hu-man
in·iq-uity
ini-tial
ini-tialed

ini-tial·ing
ini-tially
ini-ti·ate
ini-ti-ated
ini-ti-at·ing

ini-tia-tion
ini-tia-tive
ini-tia·tor
in·ject
in·ject-ing

in·jec-tion
in·junc-tion
in·jure
in·jured
in·ju-ries

in·jur-ing
in·ju-ri·ous
in·jury
in·jus-tice
ink

in·laid
in·land
inlay
inlet
in·lets

in·mate
in·nate
inner
inner-spring
inn-keeper

in·no-cence
in·no-cent
in·no-cently
in·nocu-ous
in·no-vate

in·no-vat·ing
in·no-va-tion
in·no-va-tive
in·no-va-tive-ness
in·no-va·tor

in·nu-endo
in·nu-mer-able
in·ocu-late
in·ocu-lat·ing
in·ocu-la-tion

in·op-er-able
in·op-era-tive
in·op-por-tune
in·or-di-nate
in·or-ganic

in-patient
input
in·put-ting
in·quest
in·quire

in·quired
in·qui-ries
in·quir-ing
in·quiry
in·qui-si-tion

in·quisi-tive
in·roads
in·sane
in·san-ity
in·sa-tia·ble

in·scribe
in·scribed
in·scrip-tion
in·sect
in·sec-ti-cide

in·se-cure
in·se-cu-rity
in·sen-si-tive
in·sepa-ra·ble
in·sert

in·sert-able
in·serted
in·sert-ing
in·ser-tion
in--service

in·side
in·sidi-ous
in·sight
in·sight-ful
in·sig-nia

in·sig-nifi-cance
in·sig-nifi-cant
in·sin-cere
in·sinu-ate
in·sinu-ation

in·sipid
in·sist
in·sisted
in·sis·tence
in·sist-ing

in·so-far
in·so-lence
in·so-lent
in·sol-uble
in·solv-able

in·sol-vency
in·sol-vent
in·som-nia
in·so-much
in·spect

in·spected
in·spect-ing
in·spec-tion
in·spec-tor
in·spi-ra-tion

in·spi-ra-tional
in·spire
in·spired
in·spir-ing
in·sta-bil·ity

in·stall
in·stal-la·tion
in·stalled
in·staller
in·stall-ing

in·stall-ment
In·sta-matic
in·stance
in·stances
in·stant

in·stan-ta-neous
in·stan-ta-neously
in·stantly
in·stead
in·step

in·sti-gate
in·sti-gated
in·still
in·stinct
in·sti-tute

in·sti-tuted
in·sti-tut·ing
in·sti-tu-tion
in·sti-tu-tional
in·sti-tu-tion-al·ize

in·struct
in·structed
in·struct-ing
in·struc-tion
in·struc-tional

in·struc-tive
in·struc-tor
in·stru-ment
in·stru-men·tal
in·stru-men-tal·ity

in·stru-men-ta-tion
in·sub-or-di-nate
in·sub-or-di-na-tion
in·suf-fer-able
in·suf-fi-ciency

in·suf-fi-cient
in·suf-fi-ciently
in·su-late
in·su-lated
in·su-la-tion

in·su-la·tor
in·su-lin
in·sult
in·sult-ing
in·sur-abil·ity

in·sur-able
in·sur-ance
in·sure
in·sured
in·surer

in·sur-ers
in·sur-ing
in·sur-mount-able
in·sur-rec-tion
in·tact

in·tact-ness
in·take
in·tan-gi·ble
in·te-ger
in·te-gral

in·te-grally
in·te-grate
in·te-grated
in·te-grat·ing
in·te-gra-tion

in·te-gra-tive
in·teg-rity
in·tel-lect
in·tel-lec-tual
in·tel-lec-tu·ally

in·tel-li-gence
in·tel-li-gent
in·tel-li-gently
in·tel-li-gi·ble
in·tend

in·tended
in·tend-ing
in·tense
in·tensely
in·ten-si-fied

in·ten-sify
in·ten-si-fy·ing
in·ten-sity
in·ten-sive
in·ten-sively

in·tent
in·ten-tion
in·ten-tional
in·ten-tion-ally
in·ten-tioned

in·ter·act
in·ter·ac·tion
in·ter·ac·tive
in·ter·agency
in·ter·cede

in·ter·cept
in·ter·cep·tor
in·ter·change
in·ter·change·able
in·ter·col·le·giate

in·ter·com
in·ter·com·pany
in·ter·con·nect
in·ter·con·nected
in·ter·coun·try

in·ter·de·nomi·na·tional
in·ter·de·part·ment
in·ter·de·part·men·tal
in·ter·de·part·men·tally
in·ter·dis·ci·plin·ary

in·ter·di·vi·sion
in·ter·est
in·ter·ested
in·ter·est·ing
in·ter·est·ingly

in·ter·face
in·ter·faces
in·ter·fac·ing
in·ter·fere
in·ter·fered

in·ter·fer·ence
in·ter·fer·ences
in·ter·fer·ing
in·ter·gov·ern·ment
in·terim

in·te·rior
in·te·ri·or·iza·tion
in·ter·jec·tion
in·ter·lock
in·ter·locu·tory

in·ter·lude
in·ter·me·di·ary
in·ter·me·di·ate
in·ter·min·gle
in·ter·mis·sion

in·ter·mit·tent
in·ter·mit·tently
in·ter·modal
in·ter·moun·tain
in·tern

in·ter·nal
in·ter·nal·ize
in·ter·nally
in·ter·na·tional
in·ter·na·tion·al·ize

in·ter·na·tion·ally
in·terned
in·ter·nist
in·tern·ship
in·ter·of·fice

in·ter·per·sonal
in·ter·plane·tary
in·ter·plant
in·ter·po·late
in·ter·pret

in·ter·pre·ta·tion
in·ter·pre·ta·tive
in·ter·preted
in·ter·preter
in·ter·pret·ing

in·ter·pre·tive
in·ter·re·gion
in·ter·re·lated
in·ter·re·la·tion·ship
in·ter·ro·gate

in·ter·ro·ga·tion
in·ter·roga·to·ries
in·ter·roga·tory
in·ter·rupt
in·ter·rupted

in·ter·rupt·ing
in·ter·rup·tion
in·ter·scho·las·tic
in·ter·sect
in·ter·sect·ing

in·ter·sec·tion
in·ter·sec·tional
in·ter·sperse
in·ter·state
in·ter·stel·lar

in·ter·sys·tem
in·ter·val
in·ter·vene
in·ter·vened
in·ter·ven·ing

in·ter·ven·tion
in·ter·ven·tion·ist
in·ter·view
in·ter·viewed
in·ter·viewee

in·ter·viewer
in·ter·view·ing
in·ter·weave
in·ter·wo·ven
in·tes·tate

in·tes·ti·nal
in·tes·tines
in·ti·macy
in·ti·mate
in·ti·mately

in·timi·date
in·timi·da·tion
into
in·tol·er·able
in·tol·er·ance

in·tol·er·ant
in·toxi·cate
in·toxi·cated
in·toxi·ca·tion
in·trac·ta·ble

in•tra-gov-ern-men•tal
in•tra-mu•ral
in•tra-of-fice
in•tra-squad
in•tra-state

in•tra-ve-nous
in•tri-ca-cies
in•tri-cacy
in•tri-cate
in•trigue

in•trigued
in•trigu-ing
in•trin-sic
in•trin-si-cally
in•tro-duce

in•tro-duced
in•tro-duces
in•tro-duc•ing
in•tro-duc-tion
in•tro-duc-tory

in•tro-spect
in•tro-spec-tion
in•tro-vert
in•trude
in•tru-sion

in•tru-sive
in•tu-ition
in•un-date
in•un-dated
inure

in•ured
in•vade
in•vaded
in•vad-ers
in•va-lid

in•valid *(not valid)*
in•vali-date
in•vali-dat•ing
in•vali-da-tion
in•va-lid•ity

in•valu-able
in•vari-ably
in•va-sion
in•vent
in•vented

in•ven-tion
in•ven-tive
in•ven-tor
in•ven-to-ried
in•ven-to-ries

in•ven-tory
in•ven-to-ry•ing
in•verse
in•ver-sion
in•vert

in•verted
in•vest
in•vest-able
in•vested
in•ves-ti-gate

in•ves-ti-gated
in•ves-ti-gat•ing
in•ves-ti-ga-tion
in•ves-ti-ga-tive
in•ves-ti-ga•tor

in•ves-ti-ga-tory
in•vest-ing
in•vest-ment
in•ves-tor
in•vigo-rate

in•vin-ci•ble
in•visi-bil•ity
in•vis-ible
in•vi-ta-tion
in•vi-ta-tional

in•vite
in•vited
in•vi-tee
in•vit-ing
in•vo-ca-tion

in•voice
in•voiced
in•voices
in•voic-ing
in•voke

in•voked
in•vol-un-tarily
in•vol-un-tary
in•vo-lute
in•volve

in•volved
in•volve-ment
in•volv-ing
in•ward
in•wardly

io•dine
ion-iz•ing
iono-sphere
iota
Iowa

iri-des-cence
iri-des-cent
iron
ironed
iron-ers

iron-ical
ironi-cally
iron-ing
iron-worker
ir•radi-cably

ir•ra-tio•nal
ir•regu-lar
ir•regu-lari-ties
ir•regu-lar•ity
ir•rele-vant

ir•re-place-able
ir•re-sist-ible
ir•re-spec-tive
ir•re-spon-si•ble
ir•revo-ca•ble

ir•ri-gate
ir•ri-ga-tion
ir•ri-ta-bil•ity
ir•ri-ta•ble
ir•ri-tant

ir•ri-tate
ir•ri-tated
ir•ri-tat•ing
ir•ri-ta-tion
is

is•land
isn't
iso-late
iso-lated
iso-lat•ing

iso-la-tion
is•su-ance
is•su-ances
issue
is•sued

is•suer
is•su-ing
it
italic
itali-cize

itch-ing
item
item-iza-tion
item-ize
item-ized

item-izes
item-iz•ing
it•era-tion
itin-er•ant
itin-er-ar•ies

itin-er•ary
its
it•self
I've
ivory

___ **J** _____

jacket
jack-ets
jag•ged
jail
jailed

jamb
jam-bo•ree
jammed
jam-ming
jani-tor

jani-to-rial
Janu-ary
jar
jar•gon
jaun-dice

jeal-ous
jeans
jelled
jelly
jelly-bean

jeop-ar-dize
jeop-ar-dized
jeop-ar-diz•ing
jeop-ardy
jer•sey

jet
jet-liner
jet-stream
jewel
jew-eler

jew-elry
jew•els
jiffy
jin•gle
jitter-bug

job
job•ber
job-bing
job-less
job-less-ness

jockey
jocu-lar
join
joined
join-ing

joint
jointly
joke
joker
jot

jour-nal
jour-nal•ism
jour-nal•ist
jour-nal-is•tic
jour-nal•ize

jour-ney
jo•vial
joy
joy•ful
joy•ous

ju•bi-lant
ju•bi-lee
judge
judged
judges

judg-ing
judg-ment
ju•di-cial
ju•di-ciary
ju•di-cious

ju•di-ciously
juice
juices
July
jump

jumped
jumper
jump-ing
junc-tion
junc-ture

June
jun•gle
ju•nior
junk-yard
ju•ries

ju•ris-dic-tion
ju•ris-dic-tional
ju•ris-pru-dence
ju•rist
juror

ju•rors
jury
just
jus-tice
jus-tices

jus-ti-fi-able
jus-ti-fi-ably
jus-ti-fi-ca-tion
jus-ti-fied
jus-ti-fies

jus-tify
jus-ti-fy•ing
justly
ju•ve-nile
jux-ta-po-si-tion

_K_____

ka•lei-do-scope
kan-ga•roo
Kan•sas
ka•rate
keen

keenly
keep
keeper
keep-ing
keep-sake

ken•nel
Ken-tucky
kept
ker•nel
kero-sene

ket•tle
key
key-board
key-boarding
keyed

key•ing
key-note
key-punch
key-punching
khaki

kick
kick-back
kicked
kicker
kick-ing

kick-off
kid
kid•ded
kid-ding
kid•nap

kid-napped
kid-nap•per
kid•ney
kill
killed

killer
kill-ing
ki•lo-gram
ki•lo-hertz
ki•lo-watt

ki•mono
kind
kin-der-gar•ten
kin-der-gart•ner
kind-est

kindly
kind-ness
kind-nesses
kin-dred
ki•ne-scope

kin-es-thetic
king
king-dom
kiss
kiss-ing

kit
kitchen
kitch-en-ette
kit•ten
knee

knew
knick-knack
knife
knit
knit-ted

knit-ting
knives
knob
knock
knock-down

knocked
knock-ing
knock-out
knot
knot-ted

knotty
know
know--how
know-ing
know-ingly

J
K

knowl-edge
knowl-edge-able
known
knuckle
kudos

_L_

lab
label
la•beled
la•bel-ing
labor

labo-ra-to-ries
labo-ra-tory
la•bored
la•borer
la•bor-ing

la•bo-ri•ous
la•bo-ri•ously
la•bors
lac-er•ate
lac-era-tion

lack
lacka-dai-si•cal
lacked
lack-ing
lac-quer

lac-quered
lad•der
laden
la•dies
lad•ing

lady
lag
lag-gard
lag-ging
la•goon

laid
laity
lake
lake-shore
lake-side

la•ment
la•men-ta•ble
lam-en-ta-tion
lami-nate
lami-nated

lami-nat•ing
lami-na-tion
lamp
lamp-shade
land

landed
land-fill
land-holder
land-ing
land-lady

land-lord
land-mark
land-owner
land-scape
land-scaped

land-scap•ing
land-slide
lane
lan-guage
lan-guages

lan-guish
lano-lin
lan-tern
lap belt
lapi-dary

lapped
lap-ping
lapse
lapsed
lapses

lar-ceny
large
largely
larger
larg-est

lar•vae
lar-yn-gi•tis
lar•ynx
laser
last

lasted
last-ing
lastly
latch
latches

latch-ing
late
lately
late-ness
la•tent

later
lat-eral
lat-er-ally
lat•est
latex

lathe
lather
lati-tude
lati-tu-di•nal
lat•ter

laud-able
laugh
laugh-able
laugh-ing
laugh-ter

launch
launched
launches
launch-ing
laun-der

laun-dered
laun-dries
laun-dry
lava-tory
lav-en•der

lav•ish
law
law•ful
law-fully
law-maker

lawn
law-suit
law•yer
lax
laxa-tive

lay
layer
lay•ing
lay•off
lay•out

lay-over
la•zi-ness
lazy
leach-ing
lead

leaded
leader
lead-ers
lead-er-ship
lead-ing

lead-worker
leaf-let
league
leak
leak-age

leaked
leak-ing
leaky
lean
lean-ing

lean--to
leap
leap-ing
learn
learned

learner
learn-ing
lease
leased
lease-holder

leases
leas-ing
least
leather
leather-craft

leather-neck
leave
leav-ing
lec-ture
lec-turer

lec-tur•ers
led
ledge
led•ger
led-gers

lee•way
left
left-ist
left-over
leg

leg•acy
legal
le•gal-ese
le•gal-is•tic
le•gali-ties

le•gal-ity
le•gal-iza-tion
le•gal-ize
le•gal-ized
le•gal-iz•ing

le•gally
leg•end
leg-end•ary
legi-bil•ity
leg-ible

leg-ibly
le•gion
leg-is-late
leg-is-lated
leg-is-la-tion

leg-is-la-tive
leg-is-la•tor
leg-is-la-ture
le•giti-macy
le•giti-mate

le•gume
leg-work
lei-sure
lei-surely
lemon

lem•ons
lend
lender
lend-ers
lend-ing

length
lengthen
length-ened
length-wise
lengthy

le•niency
le•nient
lens
lenses
leop-ard

leo-tard
le•sion
less
les•see
lessen

L

less-ened
less-en·ing
lesser
les·son
les·sor

let
let-down
le·thal
le·thar-gic
leth-argy

let·ter
let-tered
letter-head
let-ter·ing
let-ting

let-tuce
leu-ke·mia
levee
level
lev-eled

lev-el·ing
lev·els
lever
le·ver-age
lev·ied

lev·ies
lev·ity
levy
levy-ing
lexi-con

lia-bili-ties
lia-bil·ity
li·able
li·ai-son
libel

li·bel-ous
lib-eral
lib-er-al·ism
lib-er-al-iza-tion
lib-er-al·ize

lib-er-al-ized
lib-er-al-iz·ing
lib-er-ally
lib-er·ate
lib-era-tion

lib-erty
li·brar-ian
li·brar-ies
li·brary
li·cense

li·censed
li·censee
li·cens-ees
li·censer
li·censes

li·cens-ing
li·cen-sure
licked
lick-ing
lico-rice

lie
lied
lien
lieu
lieu-ten·ant

life
life-guard
life-long
life-saver
life--style

life-time
lift
lifted
lift-ing
liga-ment

li·ga-tion
light
lighted
lighten
ligh-ter

light-house
light-ing
lightly
light-ning
light-weight

lik-able
like
liked
like-li-hood
likely

liken
like-ness
like-wise
lik·ing
limb

lim·ber
limbo
lime
lime-ade
lime-light

lim-er·ick
lime-stone
limit
limi-ta-tion
lim-ited

lim-it·ing
lim-it-less
lim·its
lim-ou-sine
lin·age

line
lin·eal
lin·ear
lined
linen

lin·ens
liner
lin·ers
lineup
lin·ger

lin-ge·rie
lin-ger·ing
lin-guist
lin-guis·tic
lin-guists

lini-ment
lin·ing
link
link-age
link-ages

linked
link-ing
li·no-leum
lint
lip

lip-stick
liq-ue-fac-tion
liq-ue-fied
liq-uefy
liq·uid

liq-ui-date
liq-ui-dated
liq-ui-dat·ing
liq-ui-da-tion
liq-ui-da·tor

li·quid-ity
li·quor
list
listed
lis·ten

lis-tened
lis-tener
lis-ten·ing
list-ing
list-less

lit
lit·any
liter
lit-er·acy
lit-eral

lit-er-ally
lit-er·ary
lit-er·ate
lit-era-ture
litho-graph

liti-gate
liti-ga-tion
lit·ter
litter-bug
lit·tle

lit-urgy
liv-abil·ity
live
lived
live-li-hood

lively
liven
liver
live-stock
livid

liv·ing
liz·ard
lo
load
loaded

loader
load-ing
loaf
loaf-ers
loaf-ing

loan
loaned
loaner
loan-ing
loathe

loath-ing
loaves
lob-bies
lobby
lob-by·ing

lob-by·ist
local
lo·cale
lo·cali-ties
lo·cal-ity

lo·cal-iza-tion
lo·cal-ize
lo·cal-ized
lo·cally
lo·cate

lo·cated
lo·cat-ing
lo·ca-tion
lo·ca-tor
lock

locked
locker
lock-ers
lock-ing
lock-out

lock-smith
lo·co-mo-tion
lo·co-mo-tive
lo·cust
lodge

lodges
lodg-ing
loft
log
loga-rithm

loges
logged
log·ger
log-ging
logic

log-ical
logi-cally
lo·gis-ti·cal
lo·gis-ti-cally
lo·gis-tics

logo
loi·ter
lol-li·pop
lone-li-ness
lonely

lone-some
long
lon·ger
lon-gest
lon-gev·ity

long-hand
lon-gi-tude
lon-gi-tu-di·nal
lon-gi-tu-di-nally
long--standing

look
looked
look-ing
look-out
loop

looped
loop-hole
loose
loose--leaf
loosely

loosen
loos-en·ing
loos-ens
lop-sided
lo·qua-cious

lord
lose
loser
los·ers
loses

los·ing
loss
losses
lost
lot

lot-tery
loud
louder
loud-speaker
Loui-si·ana

lounge
lounges
louse
lousy
lou·ver

lov-able
love
loved
love-li-ness
lovely

lover
lov·ing
low
lower
low-ered

low-er·ing
low·est
low-land
loyal
loy-ally

loy-alty
lu·bri-cant
lu·bri-cate
lu·bri-cated
lu·bri-cat·ing

lu·bri-ca-tion
lu·bric-ity
lucid
luck
luck-ily

lucky
lu·cra-tive
lu·di-crous
lug
lug-gage

lug-ging
luke-warm
lul-laby
lum·bar
lum·ber

lum-ber·ing
lumber-jack
lu·mi-naire
lu·mi-nance
lu·mi-nary

lu·mi-nes-cence
lu·mi-nes-cent
lu·mi-nous
lump
lumped

lu·nacy
lunar
lu·na-tic
lunch
lun-cheon

lunches
lunch-room
lus-cious
lus·ter
lus-ter-less

luxu-ri·ant
luxu-ri·ous
lux·ury
ly·ceum
lying

lymph
lyr-ical
lyri-cist

_M_____

ma·ca-bre
maca-roni
ma·chete
ma·chine
ma·chin-ery

ma·chin·ing
ma·chin·ist
mac·ro·mo·lecu·lar
mac·ro·mole·cule
mad

mad-den·ing
made
mad-ness
mae-stro
maga-zine

magic
mag·ical
mag·is-trate
mag-nani-mous
mag-nate

mag-ne-sium
mag·net
mag-netic
mag-ne-tize
mag-ni-fi-ca-tion

mag-nifi-cence
mag-nifi-cent
mag-ni-fied
mag-nify
mag-ni-tude

ma·hog-any
mail
mail-able
mail-box
mailed

mailer
mail-ers
mail-ing
mail-room
main

Maine
main-frame
main-land
main-line
mainly

main-stay
main-stream
main-streaming
main-tain
main-tained

main-tain·ing
main-te-nance
ma·jes-tic
major
ma·jor-ing

ma·jor-ity
ma·jors
make
maker
mak·ers

make-shift
makeup
mak·ing
mal-ad-just-ment
mal·ady

mal-aise
mala-prop·ism
ma·laria
mal-con-tent
male

mal-fea-sance
mal-func-tion
mal-func-tioned
mal·ice
ma·li-cious

ma·lig-nancy
ma·lig-nant
ma·lin-ger
ma·lin-ger·ing
mall

mal-lea·ble
mal·let
mal-nu-tri-tion
mal-prac-tice
mam·mal

mam-moth
man
man-acle
man·age
man-age-able

man-aged
man-age-ment
man-ager
mana-ge-rial
man-ag·ers

man-ages
man-ag·ing
man-date
man-dated
man-dat·ing

man-da-tory
ma·neu-ver
ma·neu-ver-abil·ity
ma·neu-vered
ma·neu-ver·ing

man·gle
mania
ma·niac
mani-cure
mani-fest

mani-fes-ta-tion
mani-fested
mani-festo
mani-fold
ma·nila

ma·nipu-late
ma·nipu-lat·ing
ma·nipu-la-tion
ma·nipu-la-tive
man·ner

man-nered
man-ner·ism
man-nerly
man-sion
man-slaughter

M

man·tel
man·tle
man·ual
manu-ally
manu-als

manu-fac-ture
manu-fac-tured
manu-fac-turer
manu-fac-tur·ing
manu-script

many
map
maple
map-ping
mara-thon

mar·ble
March
march-ing
mar-ga-rine
mar·gin

mar-ginal
mar-gin-ally
mari-gold
ma·rina
mari-nate

mari-nated
ma·rine
mari-ner
mari-onette
mari-tal

mari-time
mark
mark-down (n.)
marked
mark-edly

marker
mark-ers
mar·ket
mar-ket-abil·ity
mar-ket-able

mar-keted
mar-ket·ing
market-place
mark-ing
markup (n.)

mar-ma-lade
ma·roon
mar-quee
marred
mar-riage

mar-riage-able
mar-ried
mar-ries
mar-ring
marry

marsh
mar-shal
mar-shal·ing
marsh-mal·low
mart

mar-tial
mar·tyr
mar·vel
mar-vel·ous
Mary-land

mas-cu-line
mask
masked
mask-ing
Ma·son-ite

ma·sonry
mas-quer·ade
mass
Mas-sa-chu-setts
mas-sa·cre

mas-sage
mas-saged
massed
masses
mas-sive

mas-tec-tomy
mas·ter
mas-tered
mas-ter·ful
master-mind

master-piece
mas-tery
match
matched
matches

match-ing
match-less
mate
ma·te-rial
ma·te-ri-al·ize

ma·te-ri-ally
ma·te-ri·als
ma·ter-nal
ma·ter-nity
math

mathe-mat-ical
mathe-ma-ti-cian
mathe-mat·ics
mati-nee
mat·ing

ma·tricu-late
ma·tricu-la-tion
mat-ri-mo-nial
ma·trix
mat·ter

mat-tress
mat-tresses
matu-rate
matu-ra-tion
matu-ra-tional

ma·ture
ma·tured
ma·tur-ing
ma·tu-rity
mav-er·ick

maxim
maxi-mal
maxi-mize
maxi-mizes
maxi-miz•ing

maxi-mum
may
maybe
may•hem
may-on-naise

mayor
may•ors
me
meadow
mea•ger

meal
mean
me•an-der
mean-ing
mean-ing•ful

mean-ing-fully
mean-ing-less
meant
mean-time
mean-while

mea-sles
mea-sur-able
mea-sure
mea-sured
mea-sure-ment

mea-sur•ing
meat
meat-ball
me•chanic
me•chan-ical

me•chani-cally
me•chan-ics
mecha-nism
mecha-nist
mecha-ni-za-tion

mecha-nize
mecha-nized
medal
med-al•ist
me•dal-lion

med•dle
media
me•dian
me•di-ate
me•dia-tion

me•dia-tor
medic
med-ical
medi-cally
medi-care

medi-cate
medi-cated
medi-ca-tion
me•dici-nal
medi-cine

me•di-eval
me•dio-cre
me•di-oc-rity
medi-tate
medi-ta-tion

medi-ta-tive
me•dium
med•ley
meet
meet-ing

mega-phone
mega-watt
mel-an-cho•lia
mel-an-choly
mel•low

me•lo-di•ous
melo-drama
mel•ody
melt
melted

melt-ing
mem•ber
mem-ber-ship
mem-brane
me•mento

memo
mem-oirs
memo-ra•ble
memo-randa
memo-ran•dum

me•mo-rial
me•mo-ri-al•ize
memo-ries
memo-rize
mem•ory

men
men•ace
mend
mend-ing
me•nial

meno-pause
men•tal
men-tal•ity
men-tally
men-tion

men-tioned
men-tion•ing
menu
mer-can-tile
mer-ce-nary

mer-cer•ize
mer-cer-ized
mer-chan-dise
mer-chan-dised
mer-chan-diser

mer-chan-dis•ing
mer-chant
mer-chant-able
mer-ci•ful
mer-ci-less

mer-cury
mercy
mere
merely
mer•est

merge
merged
merger
merg-ers
merges

merg-ing
me•rid-ian
merit
mer-ited
meri-to-ri•ous

mer•its
mer-ri•est
mer-ri-ment
merry
mess

mes-sage
mes-sages
mes-sen•ger
met
meta-bolic

me•tabo-lism
metal
me•tal-lic
met-al-lur•gic
met-al-lur-gi•cal

met-al-lur-gi-cally
met-al-lur-gist
met-al-lurgy
met•als
metal-working

meta-phor
meta-phys•ics
me•teor
me•teo-ro-logic
me•teo-ro-log-ical

me•teo-rol•ogy
meter
me•tered
me•ter-ing
me•ters

meth-ane
method
me•thod-ical
meth-od-olo-gies
meth-od-ol•ogy

meth-ods
me•ticu-lous
me•ticu-lously
met•ric
metro

met-ro-poli•tan
met•tle
mez-za-nine
mice
Michi-gan

mi•crobes
mi•cro-bi-ol•ogy
mi•cro-cas-sette
mi•cro-copy
mi•cro-farad

mi•cro-fiche
mi•cro-film
mi•cro-filmed
mi•cro-film•ing
mi•cro-flora

mi•cro-form
mi•cro-groove
mi•cro-inches
mi•crome-ter
mi•cro-me•ter *(unit)*

mi•cron
mi•cro-phone
mi•cro-pro-cess•ing
mi•cro-pro-ces•sor
mi•cro-scope

mi•cro-scopic
mi•cro-sec•ond
mi•cro-sec-tion
mi•cro-struc-ture
mi•cro-wave

mid
mid•air
mid-af•ter-noon
mid•day
mid•dle

mid-land
mid-night
mid-point
mid-range
mid-riff

mid-seg-ment
mid-se•mes•ter
midst
mid-stream
mid-term

mid•way
Mid-west
Mid-western
mid-year
might

might-ily
mighty
mi•graine
mi•grant
mi•grate

mi•gra-tion
mi•gra-tory
mild
mil•dew
mildly

mile
mile-age
mile-ages
mile-stone
mi•lieu

mili-tant
mili-tary
mi·li·tia
milk
milk-ing

mill
mil-len-nial
mil-len-nium
mil·li-me·ter
mil·li-nery

mill-ing
mil-lion
mil-lion-aire
mil-lionth
mil·li-sec·ond

mill-work
mim-eo-graph
mim-eo-graph·ing
mind
minded

mind-ful
mind-ing
mind-less
mine
mined

miner
min-eral
min-er·als
min·ers
min·gle

min-ia-ture
min-ia-tur-iza-tion
min-ia-tur·ize
min-ia-tur-ized
mini-com-puter

mini-course
mini-mal
mini-mally
mini-mize
mini-mized

mini-mizes
mini-miz·ing
mini-mum
min·ing
min-is·ter

min-is-te-rial
min-is-tries
min-is·try
mink
Min-ne-sota

minor
mi·nori-ties
mi·nor-ity
mi·nors
mint

minus
mi·nuses
min·ute *(n.)*
mi·nute *(adj.)*
mir-acle

mi·racu-lous
mi·rage
mir·ror
mis-ad·ven-ture
mis-aligned

mis-ap·pre-hen-sion
mis-be·have
mis-be·hav·ior
mis-cal·cu-lated
mis-car-riage

mis-cel-la-neous
mis-cel-lany
mis-chief
mis-chie-vous
mis-con-cep-tion

mis-con-duct
mis-con-strue
mis-count
mis-de-meanor
mis-di-rect

mis-er-able
mis·ery
mis-for-tune
mis-giv-ings
mis-guided

mis-han-dled
mis-han-dling
mis·hap
mis-in·for-ma-tion
mis-in·formed

mis-in·ter-pre-ta-tion
mis-in·ter-preted
mis-judge
mis-judg·ing
mis-la·beled

mis-laid
mis-lead
mis-lead·ing
mis-man-aged
mis-man-ag·ing

mis-matched
mis-no·mer
mis-place
mis-placed
mis-plac·ing

mis-print
mis-quote
mis-read
mis-rep·re-sent
mis-rep·re-sen-ta-tion

mis-rep·re-sented
mis-rep·re-sent·ing
mis-routed
miss
missed

mis-sent
misses
mis-sile
miss-ing
mis-sion

mis-sion-ar·ies
mis-sion·ary
Mis-sis-sippi
Mis-souri
mis-spell

mis-spell·ing
mis-state
missy
mis-tak-able
mis-take

mis-taken
mis-tak-enly
mis·tle-toe
mis-trial
mis-trust

misty
mis-un·der-stand
mis-un·der-stand·ing
mis-un·der-stood
mis·use

mis-used
miti-gate
miti-ga-tion
miti-ga-tive
mit·ten

mix
mixed
mixes
mix·ing
mix-ture

mix--up *(n.)*
mne-monic
mo·bile
mo·bil-ity
mo·bi-li-za-tion

mo·bi-lize
mo·bi-lized
mo·bi-liz·ing
moc-ca·sin
mock-ery

mock--up
mod
mode
model
mod-eled

mod-el·ing
mod·els
mod-er·ate
mod-er-ated
mod-er-ately

mod-era-tion
mod-era·tor
mod·ern
mod-ern-iza-tion
mod-ern·ize

mod-ern-iz·ing
mod·est
mod-estly
mod-esty
modi-fi-ca-tion

modi-fied
modi-fier
modi-fies
mod·ify
modi-fy·ing

modu-lar
modu-lar-ized
modu-late
modu-la-tion
mod·ule

moisten
moist-ener
mois-ture
molar
mo·las-ses

mold
molded
mold-ing
mo·lecu-lar
mole-cule

mo·lest
mol·ten
mo·lyb-de·num
mo·ment
mo·men-tarily

mo·men-tary
mo·men-tous
mo·men-tum
mon-arch
mon-ar·chy

mon-as-tery
Mon·day
mone-tary
money
mon·ies

moni-tor
moni-tored
moni-tor·ing
mon·key
mono-cle

mono-cul-ture
mono-fila-ment
mo·nog-amy
mono-gram
mono-graph

mono-lithic
mono-logue
mo·nopo-li-za-tion
mo·nopo-lize
mo·nop-oly

mono-rail
mono-tone
mo·noto-nous
mo·not-ony
mon-ox·ide

mon-ster
mon-stros·ity
mon-strous
mon-tage
Mon-tana

month	mo•tels	movie
monthly	mother	mov•ies
monu-ment	moth-proof	mov•ing
monu-men•tal	moth-proofed	mowed
mood	motif	mower
moody	mo•tion	mow•ers
moon	mo•ti-vate	mow•ing
moon-light	mo•ti-vated	much
moose	mo•ti-vat•ing	mu•ci-lage
mop	mo•ti-va-tion	mud
mop-ping	mo•ti-va-tional	mud•dle
moral	mo•ti-va•tor	muddy
mo•rale	mo•tive	muf•fin
mo•ral-ity	motor	muf•fle
mor-al•ize	motor-cade	muf-fler
mor-ally	motor-cycle	mul-berry
mora-to-rium	motor-cyclist	mulch
mor•bid	mo•tor-ing	mulch-ing
mor-bid•ity	mo•tor-ist	mul•ti-cul-tural
mor-dant	mo•tor-ize	mul•ti-eth•nic
more	motto	mul•ti-fam•ily
more-over	mould-ing	mul•ti-fari•ous
morgue	mount	mul•ti-handi-capped
morn-ing	moun-tain	mul•ti-level
mor•tal	moun-tain•ous	mul•ti-lin-gual
mor-tali-ties	mounted	mul•ti-me•dia
mor-tal•ity	mount-ing	mul•ti-mil-lion
mor-tally	mourn	mul•ti-mil-lion-aire
mor•tar	mourn-ful	mul•ti-na-tional
mort-gage	mourn-ing	mul-ti•ple
mort-gaged	mous-tache	mul-ti-pli-ca-tion
mort-gagee	mouth	mul-ti-plied
mort-gages	mouth-ful	mul-ti-plier
mort-gagor	mouth-piece	mul-ti•ply
mor-ti-cian	mov-able	mul-ti-ply•ing
mor-tu•ary	move	mul•ti-pro-cess•ing
mos-quito	moved	mul•ti-pur-pose
most	move-ment	mul•ti-sec-tion
mostly	mover	mul•ti-sen-sory
motel	mov•ers	mul•ti-sided

mul-ti-tude
mul-ti-tu-di-nous
mul-ti-vol-ume
mum-ble
mumps

munch-ing
mun-dane
mu-nici-pal
mu-nici-pali-ties
mu-nici-pal-ity

mu-nici-pally
mur-der
mur-derer
mur-der-ous
mu-ri-atic

mur-mur
mur-mur-ing
mus-cle
mus-cu-lar
mu-seum

mu-se-ums
mush-room
music
mu-si-cal
mu-si-cian

mu-si-col-ogy
mus-ket
mus-lin
must
mus-tache

mus-tard
mus-ter
mus-tered
mu-ta-tion
muted

mu-ti-late
mu-ti-lated
mu-ti-neer
mu-ti-nous
mu-tiny

mut-ter
mut-ton
mu-tual
mu-tu-ally
muz-zle

my
myr-iad
myr-tle
my-self
mys-ter-ies

mys-te-ri-ous
mys-tery
mys-ti-cal
mys-ti-fied
mys-tify

mys-ti-fy-ing
mys-tique

N

nail
nail-ing
naive
name
namely

name-plate
name-sake
nam-ing
nap-kin
nar-cotic

nar-rate
nar-ra-tion
nar-ra-tive
nar-row
nar-rowed

nar-rower
nar-rowly
nasal
nasty
na-ta-to-rium

na-tion
na-tional
na-tion-al-ist
na-tion-al-ity
na-tion-al-iza-tion

na-tion-al-ize
na-tion-al-ized
na-tion-ally
na-tion-wide
na-tive

na-tiv-ity
natu-ral
natu-ral-ist
natu-ral-iza-tion
natu-ral-ize

natu-rally
na-ture
naughty
nau-sea
nau-se-ate

nau-ti-cal
naval
navi-ga-ble
navi-gate
navi-ga-tion

navi-ga-tor
navy
near
nearby
neared

nearer
near-est
near-ing
nearly
near-ness

near-sighted
neat
neatly
Ne-braska
nebu-lous

nec-es-sar-ily
nec-es-sary
ne-ces-si-tate
ne-ces-si-tated
ne-ces-si-tat-ing

ne-ces-si-ties
ne-ces-sity
neck
neck-lace
neck-tie

nec-tar-ine
need
needed
need-ing
nee-dle

need-less
need-lessly
needle-work
needy
ne-gate

ne-gat-ing
nega-tive
nega-tively
ne-glect
ne-glected

ne-glect-ful
ne-glect-ing
neg-li-gence
neg-li-gent
neg-li-gently

neg-li-gi-ble
ne-go-tia-ble
ne-go-ti-ate
ne-go-ti-ated
ne-go-ti-at-ing

ne-go-tia-tion
ne-go-tia-tor
neigh-bor
neigh-bor-hood
neigh-bor-ing

neigh-borly
nei-ther
nephew
nepo-tism
nerve

ner-vous
ner-vous-ness
nest-ing
nes-tle
nes-tled

net
net-ted
net-ting
net-work
net-working

neu-ral
neu-ral-gia
neu-ri-tis
neu-ro-logic
neu-ro-log-ical

neu-ro-logi-cally
neu-rol-ogy
neu-ro-physi-olog-ical
neu-ro-psy-cho-log-ical
neu-ro-psy-cholo-gist

neu-ro-psy-chol-ogy
neu-ro-sis
neu-ro-sur-geon
neu-ro-sur-gery
neu-rotic

neu-tral
neu-tral-ity
neu-tral-ize
neu-tron
Ne-vada

never
never-more
never-the-less
new
new-born

new-comer
newer
new-est
New Hamp-shire
New Jer-sey

newly
New Mex-ico
new-ness
news
news-cast

news-caster
news-letter
news-paper
news-print
news-reel

news-room
news-stand
news-worthiness
news-worthy
New York

next
nib-ble
nice
nicely
nicer

nic-est
nice-ties
nicety
niche
nickel

nick-el-odeon
nick-name
nico-tine
niece
night

nightly
night-mare
night-time
nim-ble
nine

nine-teen
nine-teenth
nine-ti•eth
ninety
ninth

nip•ple
nit-pick
ni•trate
ni•trated
ni•tro-ben-zene

ni•tro-gen
ni•tro-glyc-erin
no
no•bil-ity
noble

no•body
noc-tur•nal
noc-turne
noise
noise-less

nois-ily
no•madic
no•men-cla-ture
nomi-nal
nomi-nally

nomi-nate
nomi-nated
nomi-nat•ing
nomi-na-tion
nomi-nee

non-ab•sor-bent
non-ad•mis-si•ble
non-al•co-holic
non-ap•pli-ca-bil•ity
non-ap•pli-ca•ble

non-as•sess-able
non-as•so-ci-ated
non-ath-letic
non-at•ten-dance
non-bind•ing

non-cha-lant
non-com•mer-cial
non-com•mis-sioned
non-com-mit•tal
non-com•pe-ti-tion

non-com•peti-tive
non-com•pli-ance
non-com•pli-cated
non-con•for-mance
non-con-form•ing

non-con-form•ist
non-con•for-mity
non-con-tact
non-con•tribu-tory
non-credit

non-crit-ical
non-de•duct-ible
non-de-script
non-dis•crimi-na-tion
non-dis•crimi-na-tory

non-drink•ing
non-du•pli-ca-tion
non-du-ra•ble
none
non-en-tity

non-es•sen-tial
none-the-less
non-ex•clu-sive
non-ex-empt
non-ex•is-tence

non-ex•is-tent
non-fic-tion
non-fic-tional
non-fi•nan-cial
non-for•fei-ture

non-haz-ard•ous
non-in-ter•est
non-med-ical
non-mem•ber
non-me-tal•lic

non-op•er-at•ing
non-par-ti•san
non-pay-ment
non-pro•duc-tive
non-profit

non-re•fund-able
non-resi-dent
non-resi-den•tial
non-re•stric-tive
non-re•turn-able

non-sense
non-smok•ing
non-stan-dard
non-stop
non-tax-able

non-tech-ni•cal
non-trans•fer-able
non-union
non-vio-lence
noon

noon-time
nor
nor•mal
nor-malcy
nor-mal•ity

nor-mal•ize
nor-mal-iz•ing
nor-mally
nor-ma-tive
normed

north
North Caro-lina
North Da•kota
north-east
north-eastern

north-erly
North-erner
north-ward
north-west
north-western

nose
nos-tal·gic
nos-trum
not
no·ta-ble

no·ta-bly
no·ta-rize
no·ta-rized
no·tary
no·ta-tion

notch
note
note-book
noted
note-wor·thy

noth-ing
no·tice
no·tice-able
no·ticed
no·tices

no·ti-fi-ca-tion
no·ti-fied
no·ti-fies
no·tify
no·ti-fy·ing

not·ing
no·tion
no·to-ri·ety
no·to-ri·ous
not-with-standing

nour-ish
nour-ish-ment
novel
nov-el·ist
nov-el-ties

nov-elty
No·vem-ber
nov·ice
now
nowa-days

no·where
nox-ious
noz·zle
nu·clear
nu·cleus

nu·dity
nui-sance
nul-lify
num·ber
num-bered

num-ber·ing
nu·meral
nu·mer-als
nu·mer-ate
nu·mera-tion

nu·mera-tor
nu·meric
nu·mer-ical
nu·meri-cally
nu·mer-ous

nup-tial
nurse
nurs-er·ies
nurs-ery
nurses

nurs-ing
nur-ture
nut
nut-cracker
nu·tri-tion

nu·tri-tional
nu·tri-tion·ist
nu·tri-tious
nut-shell
nuz·zle

nylon

_____ O _____

oath
obe-di-ence
obe-di·ent
obese
obe-sity

obey
obeyed
obey-ing
obitu-ary
ob·ject

ob·jected
ob·ject-ing
ob·jec-tion
ob·jec-tion-able
ob·jec-tive

ob·jec-tively
ob·jec-tiv·ity
ob·li-gate
ob·li-gated
ob·li-ga-tion

ob·li-ga-tional
obliga-tory
oblige
obliged
oblig-ing

oblit-er·ate
oblit-er-ated
obliv-ion
oblivi-ous
ob·long

ob·nox-ious
ob·scene
ob·scen-ity
ob·scure
ob·scu-rity

O

ob•serv-able
ob•ser-vance
ob•ser-vant
ob•ser-va-tion
ob•ser-va-tional

ob•ser-va-tory
ob•serve
ob•served
ob•server
ob•serv-ing

ob•ses-sion
ob•ses-sive
ob•so-les-cence
ob•so-les-cent
ob•so-lete

ob•sta-cle
ob•stet-ric
ob•stet-ri•cal
ob•stet-rics
ob•sti-nate

ob•struct
ob•struct-ing
ob•struc-tion
ob•struc-tive
ob•tain

ob•tain-able
ob•tained
ob•tain-ing
ob•tuse
ob•vi-ate

ob•vi-ous
ob•vi-ously
oc•ca-sion
oc•ca-sional
oc•ca-sion-ally

oc•ca-sioned
oc•ci-den-tal
oc•clude
oc•cluded
oc•cult

oc•cu-pancy
oc•cu-pant
oc•cu-pa-tion
oc•cu-pa-tional
oc•cu-pa-tion-ally

oc•cu-pied
oc•cu-pies
oc•cupy
oc•cu-py•ing
occur

oc•curred
oc•cur-rence
oc•cur-rences
oc•cur-ring
ocean

ocean-front
ocean-og-ra•phy
o'clock
oc•ta-gon
oc•tago-nal

oc•tane
oc•tave
Oc•to-ber
oc•to-pus
ocu•lar

ocu-list
odd
odd•ity
odi•ous
odome-ter

odor
odor-less
of
off
of•fend

of•fended
of•fender
of•fend-ing
of•fense
of•fenses

of•fen-sive
offer
of•fered
of•fer-ing
off-hand

of•fice
of•fi-cer
of•fices
of•fi-cial
of•fi-cially

of•fi-ci•ate
of•fi-ci-at•ing
of•fi-cious
off•set
off-shoot

off-shore
off-side
off-spring
often
often-times

Ohio
oil
oily
oint-ment
okay

Okla-homa
old
old--fashioned
older
old•est

Olym-pic
om•buds-man
om•elet
omi-nous
omis-sion

omis-sive
omit
omit-ted
omit-ting
om•ni-bus

on
once
on·com-ing
one
one--fifth

one--fourth
one--half
one--tenth
one--third
one-ness

oner-ous
one-self
on·go-ing
onion
onion-skin

on--line
on·look-ing
only
onset
on·slaught

onto
on·ward
opac-ity
opaque
open

opened
opener
open-ers
open-ing
openly

open-ness
opera
op·era-bil·ity
op·er-able
op·er-ate

op·er-ated
op·er-atic
op·er-at·ing
op·era-tion
op·era-tional

op·era-tion-al-ized
op·era-tive
op·era-tor
op·er-etta
oph-thal-molo-gist

oph-thal-mol·ogy
opin-ion
op·po-nent
op·por-tune
op·por-tun·ist

op·por-tu-ni-ties
op·por-tu-nity
op·pose
op·posed
op·poses

op·pos-ing
op·po-site
op·po-si-tion
op·press
op·pres-sion

op·pres-sive
op·pres-sor
opted
optic
op·ti-cal

op·ti-cally
op·ti-cian
op·tics
op·ti-mal
op·ti-mism

op·ti-mist
op·ti-mis·tic
op·ti-mize
op·ti-mum
opt·ing

op·tion
op·tional
op·tion-ally
op·tome-trist
op·tome-try

opu-lent
or
or·acle
oral
orally

or·ange
ora-tion
ora·tor
ora-tor-ical
ora-to·rio

ora-tory
orbit
or·bit-ing
or·bits
or·chard

or·ches-tra
or·ches-trate
or·dain
or·deal
order

or·dered
or·der-ing
or·der-li-ness
or·derly
or·ders

or·di-nal
or·di-nance
or·di-nances
or·di-narily
or·di-nary

or·di-na-tion
ord-nance
ore
Ore·gon
organ

or·ganic
or·gan-ism
or·gan-ist
or·ga-ni-za-tion
or·ga-ni-za-tional

or·ga·ni·za·tion·al·ly
or·ga·nize
or·ga·nized
or·ga·niz·er
or·ga·niz·ing

or·gans
ori·ent
ori·en·tal
ori·en·tat·ing
ori·en·ta·tion

ori·ented
ori·ent·ing
ori·fice
ori·gin
origi·nal

origi·nal·ity
origi·nally
origi·nate
origi·nated
origi·nat·ing

origi·na·tion
origi·na·tor
or·na·ment
or·na·men·tal
or·nate

or·phan
or·phan·age
orth·odon·tic
orth·odon·tist
or·tho·dox

or·tho·pe·dic
or·tho·pe·di·cally
or·thot·ics
or·tho·tist
os·cil·late

os·cil·lat·ing
os·cil·la·tion
os·cil·la·tor
os·mo·sis
os·ten·si·ble

os·ten·ta·tion
os·ten·ta·tious
os·tra·cize
os·trich
other

oth·ers
other-wise
ought
ounce
ounces

our
our-self
our-selves
out
out·age

out-ages
out-board
out-bound
out-break
out-building

out-burst
out-cast
out-come
out·cry
out-dated

out-distance
outdo
out-door
outer
outer-wear

out-field
out·fit
out-fit·ted
out-go·ing
out-grow

out-grown
out·ing
out-land·ish
out·law
out-lawed

out·lay
out·let
out-line
out-lined
out-lin·ing

out-live
out-look
out-ly·ing
out-num·bered
out-paced

out-patient
out-per·formed
out-pour·ing
out·put
out-rage

out-rank
out-reach
out-right
out·run
out·set

out-side
out-sider
out-skirts
out-sold
out-spo·ken

out-stand·ing
out-stand-ingly
out-stretched
out-ward
out-wardly

out-weigh
out-weighed
oval
ova·tion
oven

over
over-abun·dance
over-age
over-ages
over-all

over-bear•ing
over-board
over-bur•den
over-cast
over-charge

over-charges
over-coat
over-come
over-com•ing
over-cooked

over-con•trol
over-crowded
over-crowd•ing
overdo
over-dose

over-draft
over-drawn
over-due
over-em•pha-size
over-flow

over-flowed
over-flow•ing
over-growth
over-hand
over-hand•ing

over-haul
over-haul•ing
over-head
over-hear
over-joyed

over-lap
over-lap-ping
over-lay
over-load
over-loaded

over-looked
over-look•ing
overly
over-night
over-paid

over-pass
over-pay-ment
over-priced
over-ride
over-rid•ing

over-rule
over-run
over-seas
over-see
over-see•ing

over-seen
over-seer
over-sight
over-size
over-sized

over-spend
over-spend•ing
over-spent
over-stock
over-stocked

overt
over-take
over-throw
over-time
over-turned

over-ture
over-uti-li-za-tion
over-view
over-weight
over-whelmed

over-whelm•ing
over-whelm-ingly
over-worked
owe
owed

owing
own
owned
owner
own•ers

own-er-ship
own•ing
ox•fords
oxi-dases
oxi-da-tion

oxide
oxi-dize
oxi-dized
oxi-dizes
oxi-diz•ing

oxy•gen
oys•ter

_P_____

pace
paced
pace-maker
paces
pace-setter

pa•cific
paci-fier
pac•ify
pac•ing
pack

pack-age
pack-aged
pack-ager
pack-ages
pack-ag•ing

packed
packer
pack-ers
packet
pack-ets

pack-ing
pact
pad
pad•ded
pad-ding

P

pad·dle	pana-cea	para-lyz·ing
pad-lock	pan-cake	para-med-ical
page	pan-creas	pa·rame-ter
pag-eant	pan-de-mo-nium	para-mount
pag-eantry	panel	para-noid
pager	pan-el·ing	para-pher-na·lia
pag·ers	pan-el·ist	para-phrase
pages	pan·els	para-ple·gia
pagi-na-tion	pan-han·dle	para-ple·gic
pag·ing	panic	para-pro-fes-sional
paid	pan-ning	para-site
pail	pan-orama	para-trooper
pain	pan-ther	par·cel
pain-ful	pan-to-mime	parch-ment
pain-fully	pan-to-mim·ist	pard-ner
pain-less	pan·try	par·don
pains-tak·ing	pants	par-don-able
pains-tak-ingly	pant-suit	par·ent
paint	paper	par-ent·age
painted	paper-back	pa·ren-tal
painter	paper-board	pa-ren-the·sis
paint-ers	paper-hanger	par-fait
paint-ing	pa·pers	par·ish
pair	paper-weight	par·ishes
pair-ing	paper-work	pa·rish-io·ner
pa·ja-mas	par-able	par·ity
pal·ace	para-bolic	park
pal-at-able	para-chute	parked
pal·ate	pa·rade	park-ing
pal·let	para-dise	park-way
pal-let-iza-tion	para-dox	par·ley
pal-let-ized	para-dox-ical	par-lia-ment
pal·lid	para-gon	par-lia-men-tar·ian
pal·lor	para-graph	par-lia-men-tary
pal-pa·ble	par-al·lax	par·lor
pal-pi-tate	para-le·gal	pa·ro-chial
pal-pi-ta-tion	par-al·lel	par·ody
pal·try	par-al-lel·ism	pa·role
pam·per	pa·raly-sis	pa·roled
pam-phlet	para-lyze	pa·rolee

par·rot
pars·ley
part
par·take
parted

par·tial
par·tial·ity
par·tially
par·tici·pant
par·tici·pate

par·tici·pated
par·tici·pat·ing
par·tici·pa·tion
par·ti·ci·ple
par·ti·cle

par·ticu·lar
par·ticu·larly
par·ties
part·ing
par·ti·san

par·ti·tion
par·ti·tioned
partly
part·ner
part·ner·ship

par·took
part--time
party
par·ty·ing
pass

pass-able
pas·sage
passage-way
pass-book
passed

pas·sen·ger
passer·by
passes
pass-ing
pas·sion

pas-sive
pass-port
pass-word
past
paste

pasted
pas·tel
pas-teur-iza-tion
pas·teur·ize
pas·teur·iz·ing

pas-time
pas·tor
pas-to·ral
pas-to-rate
past-ries

pastry
pas-ture
pas-tured
patch
patched

patches
patch-ing
pat·ent
pat-ent-able
pat-ented

pat-ently
pa·ter-nal
pa·ter-nity
path
pa·thetic

patho-log-ical
pa·tholo-gist
pa·thol-ogy
pa·thos
path-way

pa·tience
pa·tient
pa·tiently
patio
pa·triot

pa·tri-otic
pa·trio-tism
pa·trol
pa·tron
pa·tron-age

pa·tron-ize
pat·ter
pat-tern
pat-terned
pat-ting

pau-city
pause
paused
paus-ing
pave

paved
pave-ment
pa·vil-ion
pav·ing
pay

pay-able
pay-check
pay·day
payee
payer

pay·ing
pay-ment
pay·off
pay·out
pay-roll

peace
peace-able
peace-ful
peace-time
peak

peaked
peak-ing
pea·nut
peas-ant
peb·ble

pecan
pec-to-ral
pe-cu-liar
pe-cu-liari-ties
pe-cu-liar-ity

pe-cu-ni-ary
peda-gog-ical
peda-gogy
pedal
pe-dan-tic

ped-dle
ped-dler
ped-es-tal
pe-des-trian
pe-di-at-ric

pe-dia-tri-cian
pe-di-at-rics
pedi-gree
peel
peel-ing

peer
peer-less
pegged
pel-let
pel-vis

penal
pe-nal-ize
pe-nal-ized
pe-nal-iz-ing
pen-al-ties

pen-alty
pen-chant
pen-cil
pen-ciled
pen-cil-ing

pen-dant
pend-ing
pen-du-lum
pene-tra-ble
pene-trant

pene-trate
pene-trated
pene-trat-ing
pene-tra-tion
pen-guin

peni-cil-lin
pen-in-sula
peni-tence
peni-tent
peni-ten-tia-ries

peni-ten-tiary
pen-man-ship
pen-nant
penned
pen-ni-less

Penn-syl-va-nia
penny
pen-sion
pen-sive
pen-ta-gon

pen-tath-lon
pent-house
pe-nu-ri-ous
pen-ury
peo-nies

peony
peo-ple
pep
pep-per
pep-per-mint

pep-per-oni
pep-tic
per
per annum
per cap-ita

per-ceive
per-ceived
per-cent
per-cent-age
per-cent-ages

per-cen-tile
per-cept
per-cep-ti-ble
per-cep-tion
per-cep-tive

per-cep-tual
per-chance
per-co-late
per-co-lat-ing
per-co-la-tion

per-co-la-tor
per-cus-sion
per-cus-sion-ist
per diem
pe-ren-nial

per-fect
per-fected
per-fect-ible
per-fect-ing
per-fec-tion

per-fec-tion-ist
per-fectly
per-fer-vid
per-fidi-ous
per-fidy

per-fo-rate
per-fo-rated
per-fo-rat-ing
per-fo-ra-tion
per-fo-ra-tor

per-form
per-for-mance
per-for-mances
per-formed
per-former

per-form-ing
per-fume
per-func-tory
per-haps
peri-gee

peril
per·il·ous
per·ils
pe·rime·ter
peri·na·tal

pe·riod
pe·ri·odic
pe·ri·od·ical
pe·ri·odi·cally
pe·ri·ods

pe·riph·eral
pe·riph·er·ally
pe·riph·ery
peri·scope
per·ish

per·ish·able
per·jure
per·jury
per·ma·nence
per·ma·nency

per·ma·nent
per·ma·nently
per·me·abil·ity
per·me·ate
per·mis·si·ble

per·mis·sion
per·mis·sive
per·mit
per·mit·ted
per·mit·ting

per·mu·ta·tion
per·ni·cious
per·ox·ide
per·pen·dicu·lar
per·pe·trate

per·pet·ual
per·petu·ate
per·petu·at·ing
per·pe·tu·ity
per·plex

per·plexed
per·plex·ing
per·plex·ity
per·qui·site
per se

per·se·cute
per·se·cu·tion
per·se·ver·ance
per·se·vere
per·sist

per·sisted
per·sis·tence
per·sis·tency
per·sis·tent
per·sis·tently

per·son
per·son·able
per·son·age
per·sonal
per·son·ali·ties

per·son·al·ity
per·son·al·ize
per·son·al·ized
per·son·ally
per·son·hood

per·soni·fi·ca·tion
per·son·ify
per·son·nel
per·spec·tive
per·spi·ra·tion

per·spire
per·suade
per·suaded
per·suad·ing
per·sua·sion

per·sua·sive
per·tain
per·tained
per·tain·ing
per·ti·nence

per·ti·nent
per·turb
per·turbed
pe·rusal
pe·ruse

pe·rused
pe·rus·ing
per·vade
per·vaded
per·vad·ing

per·va·sive
per·verse
per·ver·sion
per·ver·sity
pes·si·mism

pes·si·mist
pes·si·mis·tic
pes·ti·cide
pes·ti·lence
pes·ti·lent

pet
petal
pe·tite
pe·ti·tion
pe·ti·tioned

pe·ti·tioner
pet·ro·chem·ical
pet·rol
pe·tro·leum
petty

phan·tom
phar·ma·ceu·ti·cal
phar·ma·ceu·tics
phar·ma·colo·gist
phar·ma·col·ogy

phar·macy
phar·ynx
phase
phased
phase-out *(n.)*

phases
phas-ing
pheas-ant
phe-nomena
phe-nome•nal

phe-nome•non
phil-an-thropic
phi-lan-thro-pist
phi-lan-thropy
phil-har-monic

phi-loso-pher
philo-soph-ical
philo-sophi-cally
phi-loso-phize
phi-loso•phy

pho•bia
phone
phone card
phoned
pho-net•ics

pho-nics
phon-ing
pho-no-graph
phos-phate
phos-pho•rus

photo
pho•to-cell
pho•to-cop•ied
pho•to-cop•ies
pho•to-copy

pho•to-copy•ing
pho•to-elec-tric
photo fin-ish•ing
pho•to-graph
pho•to-graphed

pho-tog-ra-pher
pho•to-graphic
pho•to-graph•ing
pho-tog-ra•phy
pho•to-play

pho•tos
pho•to-stat
pho•to-stated
pho•to-static
pho•to-syn-the•sis

pho•to-te-leg-ra•phy
phrase
phrased
phrases
phys-ical

physi-cally
phy-si-cian
physi-cist
phys-ics
physi-olog-ical

physi-olo-gist
physi-ol•ogy
phys-io-ther•apy
phy-sique
pia-nist

piano
pia•nos
pica-yune
pick
picked

picker
picket
pick-et•ing
pick-ing
pickle

pickup
pic•nic
pic-nick•ing
pic-to-rial
pic-to-ri-ally

pic-ture
pic-tured
pic-tur-esque
pic-tur•ing
pie

piece
piece-meal
pieces
piece-work
pier

pierce
pierced
pierc-ing
pi•geon
pigeon-hole

piggy-back
pig-ment
pig-men-ta-tion
pile
piled

pil•fer
pil-fer•age
pil-fer•ing
pil•ing
pil-lage

pil•lar
pil•low
pilot
pi•lots
pim•ple

pin
pin-ball
pinch
pinch-ing
pine

pine-apple
ping
pin-na•cle
pinned
pin-ning

pin-point
pin-pointed
pin-pointing
pin-stripe
pint

pio-neer
pio-neered
pio-neer·ing
pious
pipe

pipe-line
pip·ing
pique
piqued
pi·racy

pi·rate
pi·rat-ing
pis-ta-chio
pis·tol
pis·ton

pit
pitch
pitched
pitcher
pitches

pitch-ing
pite-ous
pit-fall
piti-ful
piti-less

pi·tu-itary
pity
pivot
piv-otal
pizza

piz·zas
piz-ze·ria
plac-ard
pla-cate
place

pla-cebo
placed
place-ment
pla-centa
laces

placid
plac-ing
pla-gia-rism
pla-gia-rize
plague

plagued
plagu-ing
plaid
plain
plainly

plain-tiff
plain-tive
plan
plane
planer

planet
plane-tar·ium
plane-tary
plan-ets
plank

plank-ing
planned
plan-ner
plan-ning
plant

plan-ta-tion
planted
planter
plant-ing
plant-wide

plaque
plasma
plas-ter
plas-tered
plas-ter·ing

plas-tic
plas-ti-cally
plas-tic·ity
plat
plate

pla-teau
plated
plat-form
plat-ing
plati-num

plati-tude
pla-toon
plat-ted
plat-ter
plau-si·ble

play
play-back *(n.)*
played
player
play-ers

play-ground
play-house
play-ing
play-mate
play-thing

plaza
plea
plead
plead-ing
pleas-ant

pleas-anter
pleas-antly
pleas-antry
please
pleased

pleases
pleas-ing
pleas-ingly
plea-sur-able
plea-sure

pledge
pledged
pledges
pledg-ing
ple-nary

plen-te•ous
plen-ti•ful
plenty
pleu-risy
pli-able

pli•ers
plot
plot-ter
plot-ting
plow

plow-ing
plug
plugged
plug-ger
plug-ging

plumber
plumb-ing
plun-der
plunge
plunger

plunges
plung-ing
plu•ral
plu-ral•ism
plu-ral-is•tic

plu-ral•ity
plu-ral•ize
plus
pluses
plu-to-nium

ply-wood
pneu-matic
pneu-mo•nia
pocket
pocket-book

pock-et•ful
pocket-knife
pock-ets
po•dia-trist
po•dia-try

po•dium
poem
poet
po•etic
po•etry

poi-gnant
poin-set•tia
point
pointed
pointer

point-ing
point-less
poise
poi•son
poi-soned

poi-son•ing
poker
polar
po•lar-iza-tion
po•lar-ize

pole
po•lice
police-man
police-woman
poli-cies

po•lic-ing
pol•icy
policy-holder
polio
pol•ish

pol-ished
pol-ishes
po•lite
po•litely
po•lite-ness

po•lit-ical
po•liti-cally
poli-ti-cian
poli-tics
poll

polled
pol•len
pol-li-nate
poll-ing
poll-ster

pol-lut•ant
pol-lute
pol-lu-tion
poly-es•ter
poly-eth-yl•ene

po•lyg-amy
poly-mer
poly-meric
po•ly-mer-iza-tion
po•ly-mer-ized

poly-pro-pyl•ene
poly-sty-rene
poly-un•satu-rated
pomp-ous
pond

pon-der
pon-der•ing
pon-der•ous
pony
pool

pooled
pool-ing
poor
poorer
poorly

pop-corn
pop•per
pop-pies
poppy
popu-lar

popu-lar•ity
popu-lar•ize
popu-late
popu-lated
popu-la-tion

popu-lous
por-ce-lain
porch
porches
por-no-graphic

por-nog-ra•phy
po•rous
port
por-ta•ble
por-tage

por•tal
por•ter
port-fo•lio
por-tion
portly

por-trait
por-tray
por-trayal
por-trayed
por-tray•ing

pose
posed
poses
pos•ing
po•si-tion

po•si-tioned
po•si-tion•ing
posi-tive
posi-tively
pos-sess

pos-sessed
pos-sesses
pos-sess•ing
pos-ses-sion
pos-ses-sive

pos-sessor
pos-si-bili-ties
pos-si-bil•ity
pos-si•ble
pos-si•bly

post
post-ado-les-cent
post-age
postal
post-card

post-date
posted
poster
pos-te-rior
pos-te-ri-orly

post-ers
post-gradu•ate
post-haste
post-hu-mous
post-ing

post-logue
post-lude
post-mark
post-marked
post-master

post-na•tal
post-paid
post-pone
post-poned
post-pone-ment

post-pon•ing
post-script
post-sec-ond•ary
post-test
post-test•ing

pos-tu-late
pos-tural
pos-ture
po•tas-sium
po•tato

po•tency
po•tent
po•ten-tial
po•ten-tially
pot-hole

pot-luck
pot-pourri
pot•ted
pot•ter
pot-tery

poul-tice
poul-try
pound
pound-age
pound-ing

pour
poured
pour-ing
pov-erty
pow•der

pow-dered
power
pow-ered
pow-er•ful
power-house

pow-er-less
pow•ers
prac-ti-ca-bil•ity
prac-ti-ca•ble
prac-ti•cal

prac-ti-cal•ity
prac-ti-cally
prac-tice
prac-ticed
prac-tices

prac-tic•ing
prac-ti-tio•ner
prag-matic
prag-mat-ical
prag-mati-cally

prai-rie
praise
praise-worthy
pray
prayer

prayer-ful
prayer-fully
prayers
pray-ing
preach

preacher
preach-ers
preach-ing
preach-ment
pre-ad•mis-sion

pre-adop-tion
pre-am•ble
pre-ar-ranged
pre-as-signed
pre-au•tho-rized

pre-bill•ing
pre-cari•ous
pre-cari-ously
pre-cau-tion
pre-cau-tion•ary

pre-cede
pre-ceded
pre-ce-dence
pre-ce-dent *(adj.)*
prece-dent *(n.)*

pre-ced•ing
pre-cept
pre-cinct
pre-cious
pre-cipi-tant

pre-cipi-tate
pre-cipi-tated
pre-cipi-tat•ing
pre-cipi-ta-tion
pre-cipi-ta•tor

pre-cipi-tous
pré•cis
pre-cise
pre-cisely
pre-ci-sion

pre-clude
pre-cluded
pre-clud•ing
pre-co-cious
pre-con-ceived

pre-con-cep-tion
pre-con-di-tion
pre-con-struc-tion
preda-tor
preda-tory

pre-de-cease
pre-de-ces•sor
pre-des-ti-na-tion
pre-des-tine
pre-de-ter-mined

pre-dica-ment
predi-cate
predi-cated
predi-ca•tor
pre-dict

pre-dict-able
pre-dict-ably
pre-dicted
pre-dict•ing
pre-dic-tion

pre-dic-tive
pre-dic•tor
pre-dis-pose
pre-domi-nance
pre-domi-nant

pre-domi-nantly
pre-elec-tion
pre-emi-nence
pre-emi-nent
pre-empt

pre-empted
pre-emp-tion
pre-emp-tive
pre-en•roll-ment
pre-ex•is-tence

pre-ex•is-tent
pre-ex•ist•ing
pre•fab
pre-fab-ri-cate
pre-fab-ri-cated

pref-ace
prefa-tory
pre•fer
pref-er-able
pref-er-ably

pref-er-ence
pref-er-ences
pref-er-en-tial
pre-ferred
pre-fer-ring

pre•fix
pre-formed
preg-nancy
preg-nant
pre-heat

pre-heat•ing
pre-his-toric
pre-judge
preju-dice
preju-diced

preju-dices
preju-di-cial
preju-dic•ing
pre•law
pre-limi-nar•ies

pre-limi-nar•ily
pre-limi-nary
pre-lude
pre-ma-ture
pre-ma-turely

pre•med
pre-medi-cine
pre-mier
pre-miered
prem-ise

prem-ises
pre-mium
pre-mi•ums
pre-mo-ni-tion
pre-na•tal

pre-nomi-na-tion
pre-oc-cu-pied
prep
pre-paid
prepa-ra-tion

pre-pa-ra-tory
pre-pare
pre-pared
pre-pared-ness
pre-par•ing

pre•pay
pre-pay•ing
pre-pay-ment
pre-plan-ning
pre-pon-der-ance

prepo-si-tion
prepo-si-tional
pre-pos-ter•ous
pre-pro-duc-tion
pre-re-cord

pre-reg-is•ter
pre-reg-is-tra-tion
pre-req-ui-site
pre-re-tire-ment
pre-roga-tive

pre-school
pre-schooler
pre-scribe
pre-scribed
pre-scrib•ing

pre-scrip-tion
pre-scrip-tive
pres-ence
pres-ent *(n., adj.)*
pre-sent *(v.)*

pre-sent-able
pre-sen-ta-tion
pre-sented
pre-senter
pre-sent•ing

pres-ently
pres-er-va-tion
pre-ser-va-tive
pre-serve
pre-served

pre-server
pre-ser-vice
pre-serv•ing
pre•set
pre-side

pre-sided
presi-dency
presi-dent
president--elect
presi-den-tial

pre-sid•ing
press
press-board
pressed
presses

press-ing
pres-sure
pres-sured
pres-sur•ize
pres-sur-ized

pres-tige
pres-ti-gious
pre-stress
pre-sum-able
pre-sum-ably

pre-sume
pre-sumed
pre-sum•ing
pre-sump-tion
pre-sump-tive

pre-sump-tu•ous
pre-sup-pose
pre-tend
pre-tended
pre-tense

pre-ten-tious
pre-test
pre-tested
pre-text
pre-tran-scrip-tion

pre-trial
pret-ties
pretty
pret-zel
pre-vail

pre-vailed
pre-vail•ing
preva-lence
preva-lent
pre-vent

pre-vent-able
pre-ven-ta-tive
pre-vented
pre-vent•ing
pre-ven-tion

pre-ven-tive
pre-view
pre-viewed
pre-view•ing
pre-vi•ous

pre-vi-ously
prey
price
priced
price-less

prices
pric-ing
pride
pride-ful
priest

priest-hood
pri-mar•ily
pri-mary
prime
primed

primer
pri-me•val
prim-ing
primi-tive
prim-rose

prin-ci•pal
prin-ci-pal•ity
prin-ci-pally
prin-ci•ple
print

print-able
printed
printer
print-ing
print-out

prior
pri-ori-ties
pri-ori-tized
pri-or•ity
pris-matic

prison
pris-oner
pris-on•ers
pris-ons
pris-tine

pri-vacy
pri-vate
pri-vately
privi-lege
privi-leged

privi-leges
prize
prized
prizes
proba-bili-ties

proba-bil•ity
prob-able
prob-ably
pro-bate
pro-ba-tion

pro-ba-tional
pro-ba-tion•ary
pro-ba-tioner
pro-ba-tive
probe

prob-ing
prob-lem
prob-lem-atic
prob-lem-at-ical
pro-ce-dural

pro-ce-dure
pro-ceed
pro-ceeded
pro-ceed•ing
pro-ceeds

pro-cess
pro-cessed
pro-cesses
pro-cess•ing
pro-ces-sion

pro-ces-sional
pro-ces•sor
pro-claim
pro-claimed
pro-claim•ing

proc-la-ma-tion
pro-cras-ti-nate
pro-cras-ti-na-tion
proc-tor
pro-cure

pro-cured
pro-cure-ment
pro-cur•ing
prod
prod-ding

prodi-gal
prod-igy
pro-duce
pro-duced
pro-ducer

pro-duc•ers
pro-duces
pro-duc-ible
pro-duc•ing
prod-uct

pro-duc-tion
pro-duc-tive
pro-duc-tively
pro-duc-tiv•ity
pro-fane

pro-fan•ity
pro-fess
pro-fessed
pro-fes-sion
pro-fes-sional

pro-fes-sion-al•ism
pro-fes-sion-al•ize
pro-fes-sion-ally
pro-fes-sion•als
pro-fes•sor

pro-fes-so-rial
pro-fes-sor-ship
pro-fi-ciency
pro-fi-cient
pro-file

profit
prof-it-abil•ity
prof-it-able
prof-it-ably
prof-ited

prof-it•ing
prof-its
pro forma
pro-found
pro-fuse

pro-fu-sion
prog-eny
prog-no•sis
prog-nos•tic
prog-nos-ti-cate

prog-nos-ti-ca-tion
pro-gram
pro-gram-ma•ble
pro-gram-matic
pro-grammed

pro-gram•mer
pro-gram-ming
prog-ress *(n.)*
pro-gress *(v.)*
pro-gressed

pro-gresses
pro-gress•ing
pro-gres-sion
pro-gres-sive
pro-gres-sively

pro-hibit
pro-hib-ited
pro-hib-it•ing
pro-hi-bi-tion
pro-hibi-tive

pro-hibi-tory
pro-hib•its
pro-ject *(v.)*
proj-ect *(n.)*
pro-jected

pro-ject•ing
pro-jec-tion
pro-jec-tion•ist
pro-jec•tor
pro--life

pro-lif-er•ate
pro-lif-era-tion
pro-lific
pro-logue
pro-long

pro-lon-ga-tion
pro-longed
prome-nade
promi-nence
promi-nent

promi-nently
pro-mis-cu•ity
pro-mis-cu•ous
prom-ise
prom-ised

prom-ises
prom-is•ing
prom-is-sory
pro-mote
pro-moted

pro-moter
pro-mot•ing
pro-mo-tion
pro-mo-tional
pro-mo-tion-ally

prompt
prompted
promptly
prompt•ing
prompt-ness

pro-mul-gate
pro-mul-gated
pro-mul-gat•ing
pro-mul-ga-tion
pro-noun

pro-nounce
pro-nounced
pro-nounce-ment
pro-nun-cia-tion
proof

proof-ing
proof-read
proof-reader
proof-reading
pro-pa-ganda

propa-ga-tion
pro-pane
pro•pel
pro-pel-lant
pro-pelled

pro-pel•ler
pro-pel-ling
pro-pen-sity
proper
prop-erly

prop-er-ties
prop-erty
proph-ecy
proph-esy
prophet

pro-po-nent
pro-por-tion
pro-por-tional
pro-por-tion-ally
pro-por-tion•ate

pro-por-tion-ately
pro-por-tioned
pro-posal
pro-pos•als
pro-pose

pro-posed
pro-poses
pro-pos•ing
propo-si-tion
propo-si-tional

propped
pro-pri-etary
pro-pri-etor
pro-pri-etor-ship
pro-pri•ety

pro-pul-sion
pro-pyl•ene
pro rata
pro-rate
pro-rated

pro-rat•ing
pro-ra-tion
prose
prose-cute
prose-cuted

prose-cut•ing
prose-cu-tion
prose-cu•tor
prose-lyte
pros-pect

pros-pected
pros-pect•ing
pro-spec-tive
pros-pec•tor
pro-spec•tus

pros-per
pros-per•ity
pros-per•ous
pros-tate
pros-the•sis

pros-thetic
prosth-odon-tics
pros-trate
pro-tect
pro-tected

pro-tect•ing
pro-tec-tion
pro-tec-tive
pro-tec•tor
pro-tégé

pro-tein
pro tem
pro-test
pro-tested
pro-tester

pro-test•ing
pro-to•col
pro-to-plasm
pro-to-type
pro-tract

pro-trac•tor
pro-trude
pro-tru-sion
proud
prouder

proudly
prove
proved
proven
prov-erb

pro-vide
pro-vided
provi-dence
provi-dent
pro-vider

pro-vid•ing
prov-ince
prov-inces
pro-vin-cial
prov-ing

pro-vi-sion
pro-vi-sional
pro-viso
provo-ca-tion
pro-voca-tive

pro-voke
pro-voked
pro-vok•ing
pro-vost
prow-ess

prox-ies
prox-im•ity
prox-imo
proxy
pru-dence

pru-dent
pru-dently
pseud-onym
psy-chi-at•ric
psy-chia-trist

psy-chia•try
psy-chic
psy•cho-analy•sis
psy•cho-ana-lyst
psy•cho-edu-ca-tional

psy•cho-log-ical
psy-cholo-gist
psy-chol•ogy
psy•cho-path
psy•cho-pathic

psy-cho•sis
psy•cho-ther•apy
psy-chotic
pu•berty
pub•lic

pub-li-ca-tion
pub-li-cist
pub-lic•ity
pub-li-cize
pub-li-cized

pub-li-ciz•ing
pub-licly
pub-lish
pub-lished
pub-lisher

pub-lish•ers
pub-lishes
pub-lish•ing
pud-ding
pud•dle

pu•er-ile
pu•er-il•ity
pull
pulled
pul•ley

pull-ing
pul-mo-nary
pul•pit
pul-sa-tion
pulses

pul-ver·ize
pump
pumped
pump-ing
pump-kin

punch
punched
punches
punch-ing
punc-tual

punc-tu-al·ity
punc-tua-tion
punc-ture
pun-gent
pun·ish

pun-ish-able
pun-ished
pun-ishes
pun-ish-ment
pu·ni-tive

pupil
pu·pils
pup·pet
pup-pies
pur-chas-able

pur-chase
pur-chased
pur-chaser
pur-chas·ers
pur-chases

pur-chas·ing
pure
purely
pur-ga-tive
pur-ga-tory

purge
purged
pu·ri-fi-ca-tion
pu·rify
pu·ri-tan

pu·rity
pur·ple
pur-port
pur-port·ing
pur-pose

pur-posely
pur-poses
purse
pur-sual
pur-su-ance

pur-su·ant
pur·sue
pur-sued
pur-su·ing
pur-suit

push
push--button *(adj.)*
pushed
push-ing
pushup

pussy-cat
put
pu·trid
put-ting
putty

puz·zle
puz-zled
pyra-mid
pyra-mided
py·ro-tech-nics

_**Q**_

quad-rant
quad-ra-phonic
quad-ri-ple·gic
qua-dru-pli-cate
qua-dru-pling

quaint
quake
quak-ing
quali-fi-ca-tion
quali-fied

quali-fier
qual-ify
quali-fy·ing
quali-ta-tive
quali-ties

qual-ity
quan-dary
quan-tify
quan-ti-fy·ing
quan-ti-ta-tive

quan-ti-ties
quan-tity
quar-an-tine
quar-rel
quar-rel-some

quarry
quart
quar-ter
quarter-back
quar-terly

quar-tet
quar-tile
quartz
qua·sar
queasy

queen
quench
quench-ing
que-ries
query

quest
ques-tion
ques-tion-able
ques-tioned
ques-tion·ing

Q

ques-tion-naire	ra·cially	rainy
quib-ble	rac·ing	raise
quick	rack	raised
quicken	racket	raiser
quicker	racke-teer	rais-ers
quick-est	racquet-ball	raises
quickly	radar	rai·sin
quick-ness	ra·dial	rais-ing
quiet	ra·di-ance	rak·ing
qui-eter	ra·di-ant	ral-lied
qui-etly	ra·di-ate	ral-lies
quilt	ra·di-ated	rally
quilted	ra·di-at·ing	ral-ly·ing
quilt-ing	ra·dia-tion	ram·ble
qui-nine	ra·dia-tor	ram-bler
quin-quen-nial	rad-ical	ram-bling
quin-tet	radio	rami-fi-ca-tion
quin-tu·ple	ra·dio-ac·tive	rammed
quit	ra·di-olo-gist	ram-ming
quite	ra·di-ol·ogy	ram-page
quit-ter	ra·dios	ram-pant
quit-ting	ra·dium	ram·rod
quiz	ra·dius	ran
quiz-zes	raf·fle	ranch
quiz-zing	raf·ter	rancher
quo·rum	rage	ran-chero
quota	rag·ing	ranch-ers
quo·tas	rag·ged	ranches
quo-ta-tion	rag-time	ran·cid
quote	raid	ran·dom
quoted	rail	ran-dom·ize
quo-tient	rail-ing	ran-domly
quot-ing	rail-road	range
	rail-roading	ranger
__R_____	rail-way	rang-ers
rab·bit	rai-ment	ranges
ra·bies	rain	rang-ing
race	rain-bow	rank
races	rained	ranked
ra·cial	rain-fall	rank-ing

ran-sack
ran•som
rapid
ra•pid-ity
rap-idly

rap•ids
rap-ping
rap-port
rap-ture
rare

rarely
rarer
rar•ity
ras•cal
rasp-berry

rat
ratchet
rate
rated
rater

rather
rati-fi-ca-tion
rati-fied
rat•ify
rat•ing

ratio
ra•tion
ra•tio-nal
ra•tio-nale
ra•tio-nal-iza-tion

ra•tio-nal•ize
ra•tio-nal-iz•ing
ra•tion-ing
ra•tios
rat•tle

rat-tling
rav•age
rav-en•ous
ra•vine
rav•ish

rav-ish•ing
raw
raw-hide
rayon
raze

razed
raz•ing
razor
re•ac-credi-ta-tion
reach

reached
reaches
reach-ing
re•ac-quainted
react

re•acted
re•act-ing
re•ac-tion
re•ac-tion•ary
re•ac-ti-vate

re•ac-ti-vated
re•ac-ti-va-tion
re•ac-tor
read
read-abil•ity

read-able
reader
read-ers
read-er-ship
read-ied

readily
readi-ness
read-ing
re•ad-just
re•ad-justed

re•ad-just-ment
re•ad-mis-sion
re•ad-mit•ted
read-out
ready

re•af-firm
re•af-fir-ma-tion
re•af-firmed
re•af-firm-ing
re•af-firms

real
re•align
re•align-ment
re•al-ism
re•al-ist

re•al-is•tic
re•al-is-ti-cally
re•ali-ties
re•al-ity
re•al-iz-able

re•al-iza-tion
re•al-ize
re•al-ized
re•al-izes
re•al-iz•ing

re•al-lo-cate
re•al-lo-cated
re•al-lo-ca-tion
re•ally
realm

re•al-tor
re•alty
reap
reaper
reap-ing

re•ap-pear
re•ap-plied
re•ap-ply
re•ap-point
re•ap-pointed

re•ap-point-ment
re•ap-praisal
re•ap-praise
rear
rear-ended

R

re•ar-ma-ment
re•ar-range
re•ar-range-ment
rea•son
rea-son-able

rea-son-able-ness
rea-son-ably
rea-son•ing
re•as-sem•ble
re•as-sess

re•as-sessed
re•as-sess-ment
re•as-sign
re•as-signed
re•as-sign•ing

re•as-sign-ment
re•as-sur-ance
re•as-sure
re•as-sured
re•as-sur•ing

re•bate
rebel
re•bel-ling
re•bel-lion
re•bel-lious

re•bound
re•bounded
re•buff
re•build
re•build-ing

re•built
rebut
re•but-tal
re•but-ted
re•but-ting

re•call
re•called
re•call-ing
recap
re•ca-pitu-late

re•ca-pitu-la-tion
re•capped
re•cap-ping
re•cap-ture
re•cap-tured

re•car-pet•ing
re•cede
re•ceded
re•ceipt
re•ceipted

re•ceipt-ing
re•ceipt-able
re•ceival
re•ceive
re•ceived

re•ceiver
re•ceiv-ers
re•ceiv-er-ship
re•ceiv-ing
re•cent

re•cently
re•cep-ta•cle
re•cep-tion
re•cep-tion•ist
re•cep-tive

re•cer-ti-fi-ca-tion
re•cer-ti-fied
re•cess
re•cessed
re•ces-sion

re•ces-sional
re•ces-sion•ary
re•charge
re•charg-ing
re•check

re•checked
re•check-ing
rec•ipe
re•cipi-ent
re•cip-ro•cal

re•cip-ro-cate
re•cip-ro-cated
reci-proc•ity
re•cir-cu-late
re•cir-cu-lated

re•cir-cu-lat•ing
re•cir-cu-la-tion
re•cital
reci-ta-tion
re•cite

re•cit-ing
reck-less
reckon
reck-oned
reck-on•ing

re•claim
rec-la-ma-tion
re•claimer
re•claim-ing
re•class

re•clas-si-fi-ca-tion
re•clas-si-fied
re•clas-sify
re•cline
re•clin-ing

re•cluse
rec-og-ni-tion
rec-og-niz-able
rec-og-nize
rec-og-nized

rec-og-nizes
rec-og-niz•ing
re•coil
rec-ol-lect
rec-ol-lec-tion

rec-om-mend
rec-om-men-da-tion
rec-om-mended
rec-om-mend•ing
re•com-mit

rec-om-pense
re·com-pres-sion
re·com-pute
rec-on-cile
rec-on-ciled

rec-on-cili-ation
rec-on-cil·ing
re·con-di-tion
re·con-di-tioned
re·con-di-tion·ing

re·con-firm
re·con-firmed
re·con-nais-sance
re·con-nect
re·con-nected

re·con-nec-tion
re·con-sider
re·con-sid-era-tion
re·con-sid-ered
re·con-sign-ment

re·con-sti-tute
re·con-struct
re·con-structed
re·con-struc-tion
re·con-struc-tive

re·con-vene
re·con-vened
re·con-ven·ing
rec·ord *(n.)*
re·cord *(v.)*

re·corded
re·corder
re·cord-ers
re·cord-ing
record-keeping

re·count
re·coup
re·couped
re·coup-ing
re·coup-ment

re·course
re·cover
re·cov-er-abil·ity
re·cov-er-able
re·cov-ered

re·cov-er·ies
re·cov-er·ing
re·cov-ery
re·cre-ate
rec-re-ation

rec-re-ational
rec-re-ation-ally
re·cruit
re·cruited
re·cruiter

re·cruit-ing
re·cruit-ment
rec·tal
rect-an·gle
rect-an-gu·lar

rec-ti-fi-ca-tion
rec-ti-fied
rec-ti-fier
rec-tify
rec-ti-fy·ing

rec·tum
re·cu-per·ate
re·cu-per-at·ing
re·cu-pera-tion
re·cu-pera-tive

recur
re·curred
re·cur-rence
re·cur-rent
re·cur-ring

re·cy-cle
re·cy-cling
red
re·deco-rate
re·dedi-cate

re·deem
re·deem-abil·ity
re·deem-able
re·deemed
re·deem-ing

re·de-fine
re·defi-ni-tion
re·demp-tion
re·de-sign
re·des-ig-nated

re·de-vel-op-ment
red-head
re·di-rect
re·dis-trict
redo

re·do-ing
re·draft
re·dress
re·duce
re·duced

re·ducer
re·duces
re·duc-ing
re·duc-tion
re·dun-dance

re·dun-dant
red-wood
reel
re·elect
re·elected

re·elec-tion
reel-ing
re·em-pha·sis
re·em-pha-size
re·em-pha-sized

re·em-ploy
re·en-list
re·en-try
re·es-tab-lish
re·es-tab-lished

re•es-tab-lish-ment
re•evalu-ate
re•evalu-ated
re•evalu-ation
re•ex-ami-na-tion

re•ex-am•ine
re•ex-am-ined
refer
re•fer-able
ref-eree

ref-er•eed
ref-er-ence
ref-er-enced
ref-er-ences
ref-er-enc•ing

ref-er-en•dum
re•fer-ral
re•ferred
re•fer-ring
re•fig-ure

re•fig-ured
re•file
re•fill
re•fi-nance
re•fi-nanced

re•fi-nances
re•fi-nanc•ing
re•fine
re•fined
re•fine-ment

re•fin-er•ies
re•fin-ery
re•fin-ing
re•fin-ish
re•fin-ished

re•fin-ish•ing
re•flect
re•flected
re•flect-ing
re•flec-tion

re•flec-tive
re•flec-tor
re•flex
re•flexes
re•for-es-ta-tion

re•form
ref-or-ma-tion
re•for-ma-tive
re•for-ma-to-ries
re•for-ma-tory

re•for-mat•ted
re•for-mat-ting
re•formed
re•form-ing
re•frac-tion

re•frac-tory
re•frain
re•frained
re•frain-ing
re•fresh

re•freshed
re•fresher
re•fresh-ing
re•fresh-ingly
re•fresh-ment

re•frig-er•ant
re•frig-er•ate
re•frig-er-ated
re•frig-er-at•ing
re•frig-era-tion

re•frig-era•tor
re•fuel
ref•uge
refu-gee
re•fund

re•fund-able
re•funded
re•fund-ing
re•fur-bish
re•fur-bish•ing

re•fur-nish•ing
re•fusal
re•fuse (v.)
ref•use (n.)
re•fused

re•fuses
re•fus-ing
re•fut-able
re•fute
re•gain

re•gain-ing
regal
re•ga-lia
re•gard
re•garded

re•gard-ing
re•gard-less
re•gency
re•gen-er•ate
re•gen-er-ated

re•gen-er-at•ing
re•gen-era-tion
re•gen-era•tor
re•gents
re•gime

regi-men
regi-ment
regi-men-ta-tion
re•gion
re•gional

re•gion-ally
reg-is•ter
reg-is-tered
reg-is-ter•ing
reg-is-trant

reg-is-trar
reg-is-tra-tion
reg-is•try
re•grade
re•gress

re·gres·sion
re·gres·sive
re·gret
re·gret·ta·ble
re·gret·ta·bly

re·gret·ted
re·gret·ting
re·group
regu·lar
regu·lar·ity

regu·larly
regu·late
regu·lated
regu·lat·ing
regu·la·tion

regu·la·tor
regu·la·tory
re·gur·gi·tate
re·ha·bili·tate
re·ha·bili·tated

re·ha·bili·ta·tion
re·ha·bili·ta·tive
re·hearsal
re·hearse
re·hearsed

re·heat
re·hire
reign
re·im·burs·able
re·im·burse

re·im·bursed
re·im·burse·ment
re·im·burses
re·im·bursing
rein-deer

re·in·force
re·in·forced
re·in·force·ment
re·in·forces
re·in·forc·ing

re·in·state
re·in·stated
re·in·state·ment
re·in·stat·ing
re·in·sti·tute

re·in·sur·ance
re·in·sure
re·in·sured
re·in·surer
re·in·tro·duced

re·in·vest
re·in·vested
re·in·vest·ment
re·is·su·ance
re·is·sue

re·is·su·ing
re·it·er·ate
re·it·er·ated
re·it·er·at·ing
re·ject

re·jected
re·ject·ing
re·jec·tion
re·joice
re·joiced

re·joic·ing
re·join
re·ju·ve·nate
re·kin·dle
re·la·bel

re·la·bel·ing
re·lapse
re·late
re·lated
re·lat·ing

re·la·tion
re·la·tion-ship
rela·tive
rela·tively
relax

re·lax·ant
re·lax·ation
re·laxed
re·lax·ing
relay

re·layed
re·lay·ing
re·lays
re·lease
re·leased

re·leases
re·leas·ing
rele·gate
rele·gated
re·lent

re·lent·less
rele·vance
rele·vant
re·li·abil·ity
re·li·able

re·li·ably
re·li·ance
re·li·ant
re·lied
re·lief

re·lieve
re·lieved
re·liev·ing
re·li·gion
re·li·gious

re·lin·quish
re·lin·quished
re·lin·quish-ment
rel·ish
re·live

re·lo·cate
re·lo·cated
re·lo·cat·ing
re·lo·ca·tion
re·luc·tance

re·luc-tant
rely
re·ly-ing
re·made
re·main

re·main-der
re·mained
re·main-ing
re·mains
re·make

re·mand
re·manded
re·mark
re·mark-able
re·mark-ably

re·marked
re·mar-ket
re·mar-ket·ing
re·marks
re·mar-ried

re·marry
re·me-dial
reme-died
reme-dies
rem·edy

re·mem-ber
re·mem-bered
re·mem-ber·ing
re·mem-brance
re·mind

re·minded
re·minder
re·mind-ers
re·mind-ing
remi-nisce

remi-nis-cence
remi-nis-cent
re·miss
re·mis-sion
remit

re·mit-tance
re·mit-tances
re·mit-ted
re·mit-ting
rem-nant

re·model
re·mod-eled
re·mod-el·ing
re·mon-strate
re·morse

re·morse-ful
re·mote
re·motely
re·mov-able
re·moval

re·move
re·moved
re·mov-ing
re·mu-ner·ate
re·mu-nera-tion

re·mu-nera-tive
re·nais-sance
renal
re·name
ren·der

ren-dered
ren-der·ing
ren-dez-vous
ren-di-tion
rene-gade

re·nege
re·ne-go-tia·ble
re·ne-go-ti·ate
re·ne-go-ti-ated
re·ne-go-tia-tion

renew
re·new-able
re·newal
re·newed
re·new-ing

re·nounce
re·nounced
re·nounc-ing
reno-vate
reno-vated

reno-va-tion
re·nowned
rent
rental
rent-als

rented
renter
rent-ing
re·num-ber
re·num-bered

re·nun-cia-tion
re·oc-cur
re·oc-cur-ring
re·open
re·opened

re·open-ing
re·or-der
re·or-dered
re·or-der·ing
re·or-ga-ni-za-tion

re·or-ga-ni-za-tional
re·or-ga-nize
re·or-ga-nized
re·or-ga-niz·ing
re·pack

re·packed
re·pack-ing
re·paid
re·paint
re·painted

re·pair
re·pair-able
re·paired
re·pair-ing
repa-ra·ble

re•pa-tri•ate
re•pa-tri-ated
re•pave
re•pav-ing
repay

re•pay-able
re•pay-ing
re•peal
re•pealed
re•peal-ing

re•peat
re•peated
re•peat-edly
re•peat-ing
repel

re•pelled
re•pel-lent
re•pent
re•pen-tance
re•pen-tant

re•per-cus-sion
rep-er-toire
rep-er-tory
repe-ti-tion
repe-ti-tious

re•peti-tive
re•place
re•place-able
re•placed
re•place-ment

re•places
re•plac-ing
re•plant
re•planted
re•plant-ing

re•play
re•plen-ish
re•plete
rep-lica
rep-li•cas

rep-li-cate
rep-li-ca-tion
re•plied
re•plies
re•plugged

reply
re•ply-ing
re•port
re•port-able
re•ported

re•port-edly
re•porter
re•port-ers
re•port-ing
re•pose

re•po-si-tion
re•posi-tory
re•pos-sess
re•pos-sessed
re•pos-ses-sion

rep-re-hend
rep-re-hen-si•ble
rep-re-hen-sion
rep-re-hen-sive
rep-re-sent

rep-re-sen-ta-tion
rep-re-sen-ta-tive
rep-re-sented
rep-re-sent•ing
re•press

re•press-ible
re•pres-sion
re•prieve
rep-ri-mand
rep-ri-manded

re•print
re•printed
re•print-ing
re•pri-ori-tize
re•pri-sal

re•prise
re•proach
rep-ro-bate
rep-ro-ba-tion
re•pro-cessed

re•pro-duce
re•pro-duced
re•pro-duc-ible
re•pro-duc-ing
re•pro-duc-tion

re•pro-duc-tive
re•pro-duc-tiv•ity
re•pro-gram-ming
re•pro-graph•ics
re•proof

re•proval
re•prove
rep-tile
re•pub-lic
re•pub-li•can

re•pu-di•ate
re•pu-dia-tion
re•pug-nance
re•pug-nant
re•pulse

re•pul-sion
re•pul-sive
re•pur-chase
re•pur-chased
repu-ta•ble

repu-ta-tion
re•pute
re•puted
re•put-edly
re•quest

re•quested
re•quester
re•quest-ing
re•quire
re•quired

re·quire-ment
re·quir-ing
req-ui-site
req-ui-si-tion
req-ui-si-tioned

req-ui-si-tion·ing
re·route
rerun
re·sal-able
re·sale

re·sched-ule
re·sched-uled
re·sched-ul·ing
re·scind
res·cue

re·search
re·searched
re·searcher
re·search-ing
re·sell

re·sem-blance
re·sem-ble
re·sem-bling
re·sent
re·sented

re·sent-ful
re·sent-ment
res-er-va-tion
re·serve
re·served

re·serv-ing
re·serv-ist
res-er-voir
reset
re·ship

re·ship-ment
re·side
re·sided
resi-dence
resi-dences

resi-dency
resi-dent
resi-den-tial
re·sid-ing
re·sid-ual

resi-due
re·sign
res-ig-na-tion
re·signed
re·sign-ing

re·sil-ience
re·sil-iency
re·sil-ient
resin
res·ins

re·sist
re·sis-tance
re·sis-tant
re·sisted
re·sist-ible

re·sist-ing
re·sis-tor
reso-lute
reso-lutely
reso-lu-tion

re·solve
re·solved
re·solv-ing
reso-nance
reso-nant

reso-nate
re·sort
re·sound
re·sound-ing
re·source

re·source-ful
re·sources
re·spect
re·spect-abil·ity
re·spect-able

re·spected
re·spect-ful
re·spect-fully
re·spect-ing
re·spec-tive

re·spec-tively
res-pi-ra-tion
re·spi-ra-tory
re·spite
re·splen-dence

re·splen-dent
re·spond
re·sponded
re·spon-dent
re·spond-ing

re·sponse
re·sponses
re·spon-si-bili-ties
re·spon-si-bil·ity
re·spon-si·ble

re·spon-si·bly
re·spon-sive
rest
re·start
re·start-ing

re·state
re·state-ment
re·stat-ing
res-tau-rant
rested

rest-ful
rest-ing
res-ti-tu-tion
res-tive
rest-less

res-to-ra-tion
re·store
re·stored
re·strain
re·strained

re•strain-ing
re•straint
re•strict
re•stricted
re•strict-ing

re•stric-tion
re•stric-tive
rest room
re•struc-ture
re•struc-tured

re•struc-tur•ing
re•sub-mis-sion
re•sub-mit
re•sub-mit•ted
re•sub-mit-ting

re•sult
re•sul-tant
re•sulted
re•sult-ing
ré•sumé (n.)

re•sume (v.)
re•sumed
re•sum-ing
re•sump-tion
re•sur-face

re•sur-fac•ing
re•sur-gence
re•sur-gent
res-ur-rect
res-ur-rected

res-ur-rec-tion
re•sus-ci-tate
re•sus-ci-ta-tion
re•sus-ci-ta•tor
re•tail

re•tailed
re•tailer
re•tail-ers
re•tail-ing
re•tain

re•tained
re•tainer
re•tain-ing
re•tain-ment
re•take

re•tali-ate
re•tard
re•tar-dant
re•tar-da-tion
re•tarded

re•tard-ing
re•ten-tion
reti-cence
reti-cent
ret•ina

reti-nue
re•tire
re•tired
re•tiree
re•tire-ment

re•tir-ing
re•tort
re•tract
re•tract-able
re•trac-tion

re•trac-tor
re•train
re•trained
re•train-ing
re•tread

re•treat
re•trench
re•trench-ment
re•trial
ret-ri-bu-tion

re-triev-able
re•trieval
re•trieve
re•trieved
re•triever

re•triev-ing
ret•ro-ac-tive
ret•ro-ac-tively
ret•ro-cede
ret•ro-ces-sion

ret•ro-fire
ret•ro-gress
retro--rocket
ret•ro-spect
ret•ro-spec-tion

ret•ro-spec-tive
re--try
re•turn
re•turn-able
re•turned

re•turn-ing
re•type
re•typ-ing
re•union
re•unite

re•us-able
reuse
re•used
re•us-ing
re•value

re•vamp
re•veal
re•vealed
re•veal-ing
rev-eille

revel
reve-la-tion
re•venge
re•venge-ful
reve-nue

re•ver-ber•ate
re•vere
rev-er-ence
rev-er-ences
rev-er•end

rev-er•ent
rev-erie
re•ver-sal
re•verse
re•versed

re•verses
re•vers-ible
re•vers-ing
re•ver-sion
re•vert

re•verted
re•view
re•viewed
re•viewer
re•view-ing

re•vise
re•vised
re•vises
re•vis-ing
re•vi-sion

re•visit
re•vi-tal-iza-tion
re•vi-tal•ize
re•vi-tal-iz•ing
re•vival

re•vive
re•vived
re•vo-ca•ble
re•vo-ca-tion
re•vok-able

re•voke
re•voked
re•vok-ing
re•volt
re•volt-ing

revo-lu-tion
revo-lu-tion•ary
revo-lu-tion•ist
revo-lu-tion•ize
re•volve

re•volver
re•volv-ing
revue
re•vul-sion
re•ward

re•warded
re•ward-ing
re•wind
re•wind-ing
re•wire

re•wir-ing
re•word
re•worded
re•work
re•worked

re•work-ing
re•wound
re•wove
re•write
re•writ-ing

re•writ-ten
re•zone
re•zon-ing
rhap-sody
rheto-ric

rhe-tor-ical
rheu-matic
rheu-ma-tism
rhine-stone
rhi-noc-eros

Rhode Is•land
rho-dium
rhyme
rhythm
rhyth-mi•cal

rib•bon
rich
richer
riches
richly

rico-chet
rid
rid-dance
rid•den
rid-ding

rid•dle
ride
rider
rid•ers
rid-er-ship

ridi-cule
ri•dicu-lous
rid•ing
rifle
rig

rigged
rig-ging
right
righ-teous
right-ful

right-fully
rightly
rigid
rig-idly
rigor

rig-or•ous
rig-or-ously
rimmed
ring
ringed

ring-ing
ring-side
rink
rinse
rinses

rins-ing
riot
ri•ot-ous
ripped
rip-ping

rip·ple
rise
risen
riser
rises

ris·ing
risk
risk-ing
risky
rit·ual

ritu-al-is·tic
rival
ri·valry
river
river-bed

river-boat
riv·ers
rivet
riv-et·ing
road

road-bed
road-block
road-way
roast
roasted

roast-ing
rob
robbed
rob·ber
rob-bery

robot
ro·bust
rock
rocked
rocker

rocket
rock-ing
rocky
rode
ro·dent

rodeo
role
roll
roll-back
rolled

roller
rol-lick·ing
roll-ing
roll-out
ro·mance

ro·man-tic
ro·man-ti-cist
ro·man-ti-cize
roof
roof-ing

rookie
room
room-ette
room-ful
room-ing

room-mate
roomy
root
rooted
rope

roped
rose
roses
ros·ter
ros-trum

ro·tary
ro·tate
ro·tated
ro·tat-ing
ro·ta-tion

ro·ta-tional
ro·tis-serie
roto-till
rot·ten
ro·tund

ro·tunda
rough
rough-age
roughen
rough-ened

rough-en·ing
rougher
roughly
rough-ness
rou-lette

round
round-about
rounded
round-ing
round table

roundup
rous-ing
route
routed
rou-tine

rou-tinely
rout-ing
rov·ing
row
row-boat

royal
roy-al-ties
roy-alty
rubbed
rub·ber

rub-ber·ize
rub-bing
rub-bish
rub·ble
ru·bella

ru·be-ola
ru·bies
ruby
ruckus
rud·der

ru·di·ment
ru·di·men·tal
ru·di·men·tary
ruf-fian
rug·ged

rug-ged-ness
ruin
ru·ined
ru·in·ous
rule

ruled
ruler
rul·ing
rum·ble
rum-mage

rumor
ru·mors
run
run-about
run-around

run-away
run-down
rung
run·ner
runner--up

run-ning
run·off
run·way
rup-ture
rup-tured

rup-tur·ing
rural
rush
rushed
rust

rus·tic
rust-ing
rus·tle
rust-proof
rust-proofing

ruth-less
rut·ted

___S___

sab-bat-ical
sabo-tage
sabo-teur
sac-cha·rin
sa·chet

sack
sac-ra-ment
sa·cred
sac-ri-fice
sac-ri-ficed

sac-ri-fic·ing
sac-ri-lege
sac-ri-le-gious
sa·cro-il·iac
sac-ro-sanct

sa·crum
sad
sad·den
sad-dened
sad·dle

sadly
sad-ness
sa·fari
safe
safe-guard

safe-guarding
safe-keeping
safely
safer
saf·est

safety
saga
sa·ga-cious
sa·gac-ity
sage-brush

sag-ging
said
sail
sail-boat
sail-ing

sailor
saint
saintly
sake
sal-abil·ity

sal-able
salad
sala-ried
sala-ries
sal·ary

sale
sales-man
sales-people
sales-person
sales-woman

sali-cylic
sa·lient
sa·line
sa·lin-ity
sa·liva

sali-vate
salmon
salon
sa·loon
salt

salted
sal-tine
salty
salu-ta-tion
sa·lu-ta-to-rian

sa·lu-ta-tory
sa·lute
sal-vage
sal-vage-able
sal-vaged

sal-vag•ing
sal-va-tion
same
same-ness
sam•ple

sam-pled
sam-pler
sam-pling
sana-to-rium
sanc-tify

sanc-ti-mo-nious
sanc-tion
sanc-tu•ary
sand
san-dal

sand-blast
sanded
sand-ing
sand-paper
sand-stone

sand-wich
sand-wiches
sandy
sane
san-guine

sani-tar•ian
sani-tar•ium
sani-tary
sani-ta-tion
sani-tize

san•ity
sapped
sap-phire
sar-casm
sar-dine

sat
satchel
sat-el-lite
sa•ti-ate
satin

sat•ire
sa•tir-ical
sati-rist
sati-rize
sati-rized

sat-is-fac-tion
sat-is-fac-to-rily
sat-is-fac-tory
sat-is-fied
sat-is-fies

sat-isfy
sat-is-fy•ing
satu-rate
satu-rated
satu-ra-tion

Sat-ur•day
sau•cer
sauces
sau-er-kraut
sauna

saun-ter
sau-sage
sav•age
sav-agery
save

saved
saver
sav•ing
sa•vory
saw

saw-dust
saw-horse
saw-mill
saxo-phone
say

say•ing
scab
scaf-fold
scaf-fold•ing
scale

scaled
scalp
scalp-ing
scan
scan-dal

scan-dal•ize
scan-dal•ous
scan-ner
scape-goat
scar

scarce
scarcely
scar-ci-ties
scar-city
scare

scare-crow
scared
scar-let
scarred
scarves

scat-ter
scat-tered
scat-ter•ing
scav-en•ger
sce-nario

scene
scen-ery
sce•nic
sched-ule
sched-uled

sched-ul•ing
sche-matic
scheme
schem-ing
schizo-phre•nia

schizo-phrenic
scholar
schol-arly
schol-ar-ship
scho-las•tic

S

school
school--ager
school-ing
schoo-ner
sci-atic

sci-at•ica
sci-ence
sci-ences
sci-en-tific
sci-en-tifi-cally

sci-en-tist
scis-sors
scoop
scoop-ful
scooter

scope
scorch
scorched
scorcher
scorch-ing

score
score-board
scored
score-keeper
scorer

scor-ing
scorn
scorn-ful
scor-pion
scoun-drel

scourge
scourg-ing
scout
scout-ing
scout-master

scrab-ble
scram-ble
scrap
scrap-book
scrape

scraped
scraper
scrapped
scrap-ping
scratch

scratched
scratches
scream
screamer
scream-ing

screen
screened
screen-ing
scrib-ble
scrim-mage

script
scrip-tural
scrip-ture
scrub
scrub-bing

scrump-tious
scru-ple
scru-pu-lous
scru-pu-lously
scru-ti-nize

scru-ti-nized
scru-tiny
scuba
scuff
scuff-ing

sculpted
sculp-tor
sculp-ture
scurry
sea

sea-board
sea-borne
sea-farer
sea-food
sea-going

seal
seal-ant
sealed
sealer
seal-ing

seam
seam-less
sé•ance
sea-port
search

searched
searches
search-ing
sea-shore
sea•son

sea-son-able
sea-sonal
sea-son-ally
sea-soned
sea-son•ing

seat
seat-belt
seated
seat-ing
sea-water

sea-worthy
se•cede
se•ces-sion
se•ces-sion•ist
se•cluded

se•clu-sion
sec•ond
sec-ond-arily
sec-ond•ary
sec-onded

second-hand
sec-ondly
se•crecy
se•cret
sec-re-tarial

sec-re-tar·iat
sec-re-tar·ies
sec-re-tary
se·crete
se·creted

se·cre-tion
se·cre-tive
sec-tar·ian
sec-tari-an·ism
sec-tion

sec-tional
sec-tion-al-iz·ing
sec-tioned
sec-tion·ing
sec·tor

secu-lar
se·cure
se·cured
se·curely
se·cur-ing

se·cu-ri-ties
se·cu-rity
sedan
se·date
se·da-tion

sed-en-tary
sedi-ment
sedi-men-ta-tion
se·di-tion·ary
se·di-tious

se·duce
se·duc-tion
see
seed
seeded

seed-ing
see·ing
seek
seeker
seek-ing

seem
seemed
seem-ing
seem-ingly
seemly

seen
seep-age
seep-ing
seer-sucker
seg-ment

seg-mented
seg-ment·ing
seg-re-gate
seg-re-gated
seg-re-ga-tion

seg-re-ga-tion·ist
seis-mic
seis-mo-graph
seize
seiz-ing

sei-zure
sel·dom
se·lect
se·lected
se·lect-ing

se·lec-tion
se·lec-tive
se·lec-tively
se·lec-tiv·ity
se·lec-tor

self
self--abasement
self--abhorrence
self--abuse
self--abusive

self--addressed
self--assurance
self--centered
self--cleaning
self--complacent

self--conceit
self--confidence
self--confident
self--conscious
self--contained

self--control
self--defense
self--destruction
self--educated
self--employed

self--employment
self--esteem
self--evaluation
self--evident
self--explanatory

self--governed
self--identity
self--important
self--imposed
self--improvement

self--incriminating
self--indulgence
self--inflicted
self--ish
self--less

self--made
self--organized
self--paced
self--praise
self--protection

self--regard
self--reliance
self--respect
self--restraint
self--righteous

self--satisfaction
self--starter
self--sufficiency
self--sufficient
self--supporting

self--sustaining
self--taught
self--worth
sell
sell-able

seller
sell-ers
sell-ing
sell-out
se•man-tics

sema-phore
sem-blance
se•mes-ter
semi-an-nual
semi-an-nu-ally

semi-au-to-matic
semi-cir•cle
semi-co•lon
semi-con-duc•tor
semi-con-scious

semi-fi•nal
semi-fi-nal•ist
semi-for•mal
semi--invalid
semi-monthly

semi-nar
semi-nary
semi-per-me-able
semi-pre-cious
semi-pri-vate

semi-pro-fes-sional
semi-re-tired
semi-skilled
semi-trailer
semi-trans-par•ent

semi-weekly
semi-yearly
sen•ate
sena-tor
sena-to-rial

send
sender
send-ing
send--off
se•nile

se•nil-ity
se•nior
se•nior-ity
sen-sa-tion
sen-sa-tional

sen-sa-tion-al•ism
sen-sa-tion-ally
sense
sensed
sense-less

senses
sen-si-bil•ity
sen-si•ble
sens-ing
sen-si-tive

sen-si-tivi-ties
sen-si-tiv•ity
sen-si-tize
sen-si-tized
sen•sor

sen-so-ri-mo•tor
sen-sory
sen-sual
sent
sen-tence

sen-tenced
sen-tences
sen-tenc•ing
sen-ti-ment
sen-ti-men•tal

sen-ti•nel
sen•try
sepa-ra•ble
sepa-rate
sepa-rated

sepa-rately
sepa-rat•ing
sepa-ra-tion
sepa-ra•tor
Sep-tem•ber

sep•tic
se•quel
se•quence
se•quences
se•quenc-ing

se•quen-tial
se•quen-tially
se•ques-ter
se•quin
sere-nade

ser-en-dip•ity
se•rene
se•ren-ity
ser-geant
se•rial

se•ri-al•ize
se•ries
se•ri-ous
se•ri-ously
se•ri-ous-ness

ser•mon
ser-mon•ize
ser-pent
ser-rate
serum

ser-vant
serve
served
server
ser-vice

ser-vice-abil•ity
ser-vice-able
ser-viced
ser-vices
ser-vic•ing

serv-ing
ser-vi-tude
ses-sion
set
set-back

set•ter
set-ting
set•tle
set-tled
set-tle-ment

set-tler
set-tling
setup
seven
sev-en-teen

sev-enth
sev-en-ties
sev-enty
sever
sev-er-able

sev-eral
sev-er-ally
sev-er-ance
se•vere
sev-ered

se•verely
se•ver-ity
sew
sew•age
sewed

sewer
sew-er•age
sew•ing
sewn
sex

sex•ist
sex-tant
sex•ton
sex•ual
sexu-al•ity

shabby
shackle
shade
shaded
shad-ing

shadow
shady
shaft
shaggy
shake

shaken
shaker
shak-ers
shak-ing
shaky

shale
shall
shal-low
shal-lower
sham-bles

shame
shamed
shame-ful
shame-less
sham-ing

sham-poo
sham-poo•ing
shanty
shape
shaped

shap-ing
share
share-cropper
shared
share-holder

share-holders
shar-ing
sharp
sharpen
sharp-ened

sharp-ener
sharp-en•ing
sharp-ens
sharp-est
sharply

sharp-shooter
shat-ter
shat-ter•ing
shatter-proof
shave

shaven
shaver
shav-ing
she
shear

sheathe
sheath-ing
shed
shed-ding
sheep

sheep-ish
sheet
sheet-ing
Sheet-rock
shelf

she'll
shel-lac
shel-ter
shel-tered
shel-ter•ing

shelve
shelved
shelves
shelv-ing
shep-herd

sher-bet
sher-iff
shield
shielded
shield-ing

shift	shor-ing	shown
shifted	short	show--off *(n.)*
shift-ing	short-age	show-room
shift-less	short-ages	shrap-nel
shin	short-cake	shred
shine	short-change	shred-ded
shin-gle	short-com·ing	shred-der
shin-ing	shorted	shred-ding
shiny	shorten	shrewd
ship	short-ened	shrine
ship-ment	short-en·ing	shrink
shipped	shorter	shrink-age
ship-per	short-est	shrink-ing
ship-ping	short-fall	shrivel
ship-shape	short-hand	shrub
ship-yard	short-handed	shrub-bery
shirt	shortly	shrunken
shirt-tail	short-ness	shud-der
shiver	short-sighted	shuf-fle
shock	shot	shuffle-board
shocked	shot-gun	shuf-fled
shock-ing	shot put	shuf-fling
shock-proof	should	shut
shoddy	shoul-der	shut-down
shoe	shoul-der·ing	shut--in *(n.)*
shoe-maker	shouldn't	shut-out *(n.)*
shoe-string	shout	shut-ter
shook	shout-ing	shut-ting
shoot	shove	shut-tle
shooter	shovel	sib-ling
shoot-ing	shov-el·ful	sick
shop	shov-ing	sicken
shop-keeper	show	sick-ened
shop-lifter	show-boat	sick-en·ing
shop-lifting	show-case	sickle
shopped	show-down	sickly
shop-per	showed	sick-ness
shop-ping	shower	sick-nesses
shore	show-ers	sick-room
shore-line	show-ing	side

side-arm *(adj.)*
side-board
side-burns
sided
side-light

side-line
side-show
side-step
side-swipe
side-track

side-walk
side-wall
side-ways
sid·ing
siege

si·esta
sieve
siev-ing
sift
sifted

sift-ing
sight
sighted
sight-less
sightly

sight--seeing
sight-seer
sign
sig·nal
sig-naled

sig-nal·ing
sig-na-tory
sig-na-ture
sign-board
signed

signer
sign-ers
sig-nifi-cance
sig-nifi-cant
sig-nifi-cantly

sig-ni-fies
sig-nify
sign-ing
si·lence
si·lent

si-lently
sil-hou-ette
sil·ica
sili-cone
sili-co·sis

silken
sills
sil·ver
silver plate
sil-ver-ware

sil-very
simi-lar
simi-lari-ties
simi-lar·ity
simi-larly

sim·ile
si·mili-tude
sim·mer
sim·ple
sim-pler

sim-plest
sim-plic·ity
sim-pli-fi-ca-tion
sim-pli-fied
sim-pli-fies

sim-plify
sim-pli-fy·ing
sim-plis·tic
sim·ply
simu-late

simu-lated
simu-la-tion
si·mul-cast
si·mul-ta-neous
si·mul-ta-neously

since
sin-cere
sin-cerely
sin-cer·est
sin-cer·ity

sin·ful
sing
singer
sing-ers
sing-ing

sin·gle
sin-gled
sin-gu·lar
sin-gu-larly
sin-is·ter

sink
sink-age
sinker
sink-ing
sin-less

sinus
si·nuses
sip
sip-ping
sir

sired
siren
sir-loin
sis·ter
sit

site
sit·ter
sit-ting
situ-ate
situ-ated

situ-ation
situ-ational
six
six--pack
six-teen

six-teenth
sixth
six-ties
six-ti•eth
sixty

siz-able
size
sized
sizes
siz•ing

siz•zle
siz-zling
skate
skate-board
skat-ing

skele-tal
skele-ton
skep-tic
skep-ti•cal
skep-ti-cism

sketch
sketched
sketches
sketch-ing
sketchy

skewer
ski
skid
skid-ded
skid-ding

skier
ski•ing
skill
skilled
skil-let

skill-ful
skill-fully
skim
skin
skin-less

skinned
skin-ning
skinny
skip
skipped

skip-ping
skir-mish
skirt
skirt-board
skit-tish

skull
sky
sky-diving
sky•lab
sky-light

sky-line
sky-rocket
sky-rocketing
sky-scraper
sky-walk

slab
slack
slacken
slack-ened
sla•lom

slan-der
slan-der•ous
slant
slanted
slant-ing

slap
slapped
slap-ping
slate
slated

slaugh-ter
slaugh-tered
slaughter-house
slav-ery
sled-ding

sleep
sleep-ing
sleep-walk
sleep-wear
sleet

sleeve
sleeved
sleigh
sleigh-ing
slen-der

slen-der•ize
slick
slicker
slide
slid-ing

slight
slighted
slight-est
slight-ing
slightly

sling-shot
slip
slip-cover
slip-page
slipped

slip-per
slip-pers
slip-pery
slip-ping
slither

sliver
slo•gan
slope
sloppy
slosh-ing

slot
slot-ted
slouch-ing
slov-enly
slow

slow-down
slowed
slower
slow-est
slow-ing

slowly
slow-ness
sludge
slug-ging
slug-gish

slum-ber
slump
slung
small
smaller

small-est
smart
smarter
smartly
smart-ness

smashed
smat-ter
smat-ter·ing
smear
smear-ing

smell
smell-ing
smelter
smile
smil-ing

smoke
smoked
smoke-house
smoke-houses
smoker

smok-ers
smok-ing
smol-der
smooth
smoother

smooth-est
smoothly
smooth-ness
smor-gas-bord
smother

smut
snack
snag
snag-ging
snap-dragon

snap-ping
snappy
snap-shot
sneak
sneaked

sneaker
sneak-ing
sneezed
sneez-ing
snob-bery

snob-bish
snow
snowed
snow-fall
snow-mobile

snow-shoe
snug
so
soak
soaked

soar
soared
soar-ing
sober
so·ber-ing

so·bri-ety
so--called
soc·cer
so·cia-ble
so·cial

so·cial-ism
so·cial-ist
so·cial-is·tic
so·ci-ali-ties
so·ci-al·ity

so·cial-iza-tion
so·cial-ize
so·cial-ized
so·cial-iz·ing
so·cially

so·ci-etal
so·ci-et·ies
so·ci-ety
so·cio-eco-nomic
so·cio-log-ical

so·cio-logi-cally
so·ci-olo-gist
so·ci-ol·ogy
so·cio-path
so·cio-pathic

socket
sock-ets
sod
soda
sod-ded

sod-ding
so·dium
soft
soft-ball
soft-cover

soften
soft-ened
soft-en·ing
soft-ness
soft-ware

soil
soiled
so·lace
solar
sold

sol·der
sol·der·ing
sol-dier
sole
solely

sol·emn
sol-em-nize
so·le-noid
so·licit
so·lici-ta-tion

so·lic-ited
so·lic-it·ing
so·lici-tor
so·lici-tous
solid

soli-dar·ity
so·lidi-fied
so·lid-ify
so·lidi-fy·ing
sol-idly

so·lilo-quy
soli-taire
soli-tary
soli-tude
solo

so·lo-ist
solu-bil·ity
solu-bi-lized
sol-uble
so·lu-tion

solv-able
solve
solved
sol-vency
sol-vent

solv-ing
som·ber
some
some-body
some-day

some-how
some-one
some-place
som-er-sault
some-thing

some-time
some-what
some-where
som-no-lence
son

sonar
song
sonic
soni-cally
soon

sooner
soothe
sooth-ing
so·phis-ti-cate
so·phis-ti-cated

so·phis-ti-ca-tion
sopho-more
so·prano
sor-cery
sor·did

sore
sorely
sore-ness
sor-ghum
so·ror-ity

sor·row
sor-row·ful
sorry
sort
sorted

sorter
sort-ing
sought
soul
sound

sounded
sounder
sound-est
sound-ing
sound-ness

sound-proof
source
sources
south
South Caro-lina

South Da·kota
south-east
south-eastern
south-erly
south-ern

south-west
south-western
sou-ve·nir
sov-er-eign
soy-bean

space
space-craft
spaced
spaces
space-ship

spac-ing
spa-cious
spa-ghetti
span
span-gle

span-gled
spar
spare
spared
spar-ing

spark
sparked
spar-kle
spar-kler
spar-kling

spark plug
sparse
sparsely
spas-tic
spa-tial

spawn
spawn-ing
speak
speaker
peak-ers

peak-ing
pear
pear-head
pear-head·ing
pear-mint

pec
pe-cial
pe-cial·ist
pe-ci-ali-ties
pe-ci-al·ity

pe-cial-iza-tion
pe-cial·ize
pe-cial-ized
pe-cial-izes
pe-cial-iz·ing

pe-cially
pe-cial-ties
pe-cialty
pe-ci·ate
pe-cies

pe-cific
pe-cifi-cally
peci-fi-ca-tion
peci-fied
peci-fies

ec-ify
peci-fy·ing
peci-men
ec-ta·cle
ec-tacu·lar

spec-tacu-larly
spec-ta·tor
spec-ter
spec-trum
specu-late

specu-lated
specu-la-tion
specu-la-tive
specu-la·tor
speech

speeches
speech-less
speed
speeded
speed-ily

speed-ing
speed-ome·ter
speed-way
speedy
spell

spell-binding
spell-bound
spelled
speller
spell-ing

spend
spend-able
spend-ing
spent
sphere

spher-ical
spher-oid
sphinx
spi·der
spike

spill
spill-age
spilled
spill-ing
spill-way

spilt
spin
spin-ach
spi·nal
spin-dle

spin-dling
spine
spine-less
spin-ner
spin-ning

spi·ral
spirit
spir-ited
spir-its
spiri-tual

spiri-tu-al·ity
spiri-tu-ally
spite
spit-ting
splash

splash-ing
splat-ter
spleen
splen-did
splen-dor

splice
splicer
splint
splin-ter
splint-ered

splin-ting
split
split-ting
splurge
spoil

spoil-age
spoil-ing
spoke
spo·ken
spokes-person

spon-sor
spon-sored
spon-sor•ing
spon-sor-ship
spon-ta-ne•ity

spon-ta-ne•ous
spon-ta-ne-ously
spool
spool-ing
spoon-ful

spo-radic
sport
sport-ing
sports-caster
sports-wear

spot
spot-less
spot-lessly
spot-light
spot-lighted

spot-ted
spot-ting
spotty
spouse
spouses

spout
sprain
sprawled
spray
sprayed

sprayer
spray-ing
spread
spreader
spread-ing

spring
spring-board
spring-time
sprin-kle
sprin-kler

sprocket
spur
spurred
spur-ring
sput-ter

spu•tum
spy-glass
squab-ble
squad
squad-ron

squalid
squan-der
square
squarely
squat-ter

squeak
squea-mish
squeeze
squeezed
squeezes

squeez-ing
squelch
squir-rel
sta-bile
sta-bil•ity

sta-bi-li-za-tion
sta-bi-lize
sta-bi-lized
sta•ble
stac-cato

stack
stacked
stack-ing
sta-dium
staff

staffed
staffer
staff-ing
stage
staged

stages
stag-ger
stag-gered
stag-ger•ing
stag-ing

stag-nant
stag-nate
stain
stained
stain-ing

stain-less
stair
stair-case
stair-way
stair-well

stake
staked
stake-out *(n.)*
stak-ing
stale-mate

stall
stalled
stal-lion
stal-wart
stam-ina

stamp
stamped
stam-pede
stamper
stamp-ing

stance
stand
stan-dard
stan-dard-iza-tion
stan-dard•ize

stan-dard-ized
stan-dard-iz•ing
standby
stand-ing
stand-point

stand-still
stanza
sta•ple
sta-pled
sta-pler

sta-pling
star
star-board
star-dom
stare

star-ing
star-light
starred
star-ring
start

started
starter
start-ers
start-ing
star-tle

star-tled
star-tling
start--up *(n.)*
star-va-tion
starve

state
stated
stately
state-ment
state-room

state-side
state-wide
static
stat-ing
sta-tion

sta-tion•ary
sta-tioned
sta-tio•ner
sta-tio-nery
sta-tion wagon

sta-tis-ti•cal
sta-tis-ti-cally
stat-is-ti-cian
sta-tis-tics
statue

statu-esque
stat-ure
sta•tus
sta•tus quo
stat-ute

statu-tory
staunch
stay
stayed
stay-ing

stead-fast
stead-fastly
steadier
steadily
steady

steak
steal
steal-ing
stealth
steam

steam-boat
steamed
steamer
steam-ers
steam-ship

steel
steel-worker
steep
steeper
stee-ple

steeply
steer
steer-age
steer-ing
stel-lar

stem
stemmed
stem-ming
sten-cil
sten-ciled

sten-cil•ing
ste-nog-ra-pher
steno-graphic
ste-nog-ra•phy
step

step-child
step-ladder
stepped
step-ping
ste•reo

ste-reo-phonic
ste-reo-type
ste-reo-typed
ster-ile
ste-ril•ity

ster-il-iza-tion
ster-il•ize
ster-il-iz•ing
ster-ling
stetho-scope

ste-ve-dore
ste-ve-dor•ing
stew-ard
stew-ard-ship
stick

sticker
stick-ers
stick-ing
stick-ler
sticky

stiff
stiffen
stiff-ener
stigma
stig-ma-tize

still
stimu-lant
stimu-late
stimu-lated
stimu-lat•ing

stimu-la-tion
stimu-la-tive
stimu-la•tor
stimu-lus
sting

sting-ing
stingy
sti-pend
stipu-late
stipu-lated

stipu-lat•ing
stipu-la-tion
stir
stirred
stir-ring

stitch
stitched
stitches
stitch-ing
stock

stock-broker
stocked
stock-holder
stock-holders
stock-ing

stock-pile
stock-piled
stock-piling
stock-room
stock-yard

stole
stolen
stom-ach
stomp
stone

stood
stooped
stop
stop-gap
stop-light

stop-over
stop-page
stop-pages
stopped
stop-per

stop-ping
stor-abil•ity
stor-age
store
stored

store-front
store-house
store-keeper
store-keepers
store-room

sto-ries
stor-ing
storm
stormy
story

story-board
story-boarding
stow-age
stowed
strad-dle

strag-gle
straight
straighten
straight-ened
straight-en•ing

strain
strained
strainer
strain-ing
strand

strange
strangely
stranger
stran-gle
stran-gu-late

stran-gu-lat•ing
stran-gu-la-tion
strap
strap-less
strapped

strap-ping
strata-gem
stra-te•gic
stra-te-gi-cally
strate-gies

strat-egy
strato-sphere
stra-tum
straw-berry
streak

streak-ing
stream
streamer
stream-line
stream-lined

stream-lining
street
strength
strengthen
strength-ened

strength-en•ing
strenu-ous
strep-to-coc•cus
strep-to-my•cin
stress

stressed
stresses
stress-ful
stress-ing
stretch

stretched
stretcher
stretch-ers
stretch-ing
stricken

strict
stricter
strict-est
strictly
strike

striker
strik-ing
string
strin-gent
stringer

string-ing
strip
stripe
striped
strip-ing

stripped
strip-ping
strive
striv-ing
stroke

strok-ing
strong
stron-ger
stron-gest
strongly

struck
struc-tural
struc-tur-ally
struc-ture
struc-tured

struc-tur·ing
strug-gle
strug-gling
strut
stub-born

stub-born-ness
stucco
stu-dent
stu-dent body
stud-ied

stud-ies
stu·dio
stu-di·ous
studs
study

study-ing
stuff
stuffed
stuffer
stuff-ing

stum-ble
stum-bled
stum-bling
stump
stun-ning

stu-pen-dous
stu·pid
stu-pid·ity
stu·por
stur-dier

sturdy
stut-ter
style
styled
styl-ing

styl-ish
sty-lis·tic
sty-mied
sty-rene
suave

sub
sub-agent
sub-area
sub-base-ment
sub-class

sub-classes
sub-com-mit·tee
sub-con-tract
sub-con-trac·tor
sub-di-vide

sub-di-vided
sub-di-vid·ing
sub-di-vi-sion
sub·due
sub-group

sub-head·ing
sub-ject
sub-jected
sub-ject·ing
sub-jec-tive

sub-ju-ga-tion
sub-junc-tive
sub-lease
sub-leases
sub·let

sub-lime
sub-ma-rine
sub-merge
sub-mis-sion
sub·mit

sub-mit·tal
sub-mit·ted
sub-mit-ting
sub-or-di-nate
sub-or-di-nated

sub-or-di-na-tion
sub-para-graph
sub-poena
sub-scribe
sub-scribed

sub-scriber
sub-scrib·ing
sub-scrip-tion
sub-sec-tion
sub-se-quent

sub-se-quently
sub-side
sub-si-dence
sub-sid-iar•ies
sub-sid-iary

sub-si-dies
sub-sid•ing
sub-si-dize
sub-si-dized
sub-si-diz•ing

sub-sidy
sub-sist
sub-sis-tence
sub-stance
sub-stances

sub-stan-dard
sub-stan-tial
sub-stan-tially
sub-stan-ti•ate
sub-stan-ti-ated

sub-stan-ti-at•ing
sub-stan-tia-tion
sub-stan-tive
sub-stan-tively
sub-sta-tion

sub-sti-tute
sub-sti-tuted
sub-sti-tut•ing
sub-sti-tu-tion
sub-strate

sub-sur-face
sub-sys•tem
sub-task
sub-ter-fuge
sub-ter-ra-nean

sub-ti•tle
sub•tle
sub-topic
sub-to•tal
sub-tract

sub-tracted
sub-tract•ing
sub-trac-tion
sub•urb
sub-ur•ban

sub-ver-sion
sub-ver-sive
sub•way
sub-zero
suc-ceed

suc-ceeded
suc-ceed•ing
suc-cess
suc-cesses
suc-cess•ful

suc-cess-fully
suc-ces-sion
suc-ces-sive
suc-ces-sively
suc-ces•sor

suc-cinct
suc-cinctly
suc-cumb
such
sucker

suc-tion
sud•den
sud-denly
sued
suf•fer

suf-fered
suf-ferer
suf-fer•ing
suf-fice
suf-fi-ciency

suf-fi-cient
suf-fi-ciently
suf•fix
suf-fixes
suf-fo-cate

suf-fo-cat•ing
suf-fo-ca-tion
suf-frage
sugar
sug-gest

sug-gested
sug-gest•ing
sug-ges-tion
sug-ges-tive
sui-cidal

sui-cide
suit
suit-abil•ity
suit-able
suit-case

suite
suited
suit-ing
sul-fate
sul-fide

sul•fur
sul•fu-rous
sul•len
sum
sum-ma-ries

sum-ma-ri-za-tion
sum-ma-rize
sum-ma-rized
sum-ma-rizes
sum-ma-riz•ing

sum-mary
sum-ma-tion
summed
sum•mer
summer-time

sum-ming
sum•mit
sum•mon
sum-moned
sump-tu•ous

sun
sun-burn
sun-burst
sun·dae
Sun·day

sun·dry
sun-flower
sun-light
sun-ning
sunny

sun-rise
sun·set
sun-shine
sun-tanned
super

su·perb
su·perbly
su·per-crit-ical
su·per-fi-cial
su·per-fi-cially

su·per-flu·ous
su·per-im-pose
su·per-im-posed
su·per-in-ten-dency
su·per-in-ten-dent

su·pe-rior
su·pe-ri-or·ity
su·per-la-tive
su·per-mar·ket
su·per-natu·ral

su·per-script
su·per-sede
su·per-seded
su·per-sed·ing
su·per-sonic

su·per-sti-tion
su·per-sti-tious
su·per-vise
su·per-vised
su·per-vises

su·per-vis·ing
su·per-vi-sion
su·per-vi·sor
su·per-vi-sory
sup·per

sup-plant
sup-plant·ing
sup·ple
sup-ple-ment
sup-ple-men·tal

sup-ple-men-tary
sup-ple-men-ta-tion
sup-ple-mented
sup-ple-ment·ing
sup-pli-ca-tion

sup-plied
sup-plier
sup-plies
sup·ply
sup-ply·ing

sup-port
sup-ported
sup-porter
sup-port·ing
sup-port·ive

sup-pose
sup-posed
sup-pos-edly
sup-pos·ing
sup-po-si-tion

sup-posi-to-ries
sup-posi-tory
sup-press
sup-pres-sion
su·prem-acy

su·preme
sur-charge
sure
surely
sur·est

sure-ties
surety
sur-face
sur-faced
sur-faces

sur-fac·ing
surf-board
surf-ing
surge
sur-geon

sur-gery
sur-gi·cal
surg-ing
sur-mise
sur-mount

sur-mounted
sur-name
sur-pass
sur-passed
sur-passes

sur-plus
sur-pluses
sur-prise
sur-prised
sur-prises

sur-pris·ing
sur-pris-ingly
sur-ren·der
sur-ren-dered
sur-ren-der·ing

sur-ro-gate
sur-round
sur-rounded
sur-round·ing
sur·tax

sur-veil-lance
sur·vey
sur-veyed
sur-vey·ing
sur-veyor

sur·viv·abil·ity
sur·viv·able
sur·vival
sur·vive
sur·vived

sur·viv·ing
sur·vi·vor
sur·vi·vor·ship
sus·cep·ti·ble
sus·pect

sus·pected
sus·pect·ing
sus·pend
sus·pended
sus·pend·ing

sus·pense
sus·pense·ful
sus·pen·sion
sus·pi·cion
sus·pi·cious

sus·tain
sus·tain·able
sus·tained
sus·tain·ing
sus·te·nance

su·ture
swab
swabbed
swab·bing
swales

swal·low
swap·ping
sweater
sweat·ers
sweat·suit

sweeper
sweep·ing
sweep·stakes
sweet
sweet·ener

sweet·en·ing
sweet·heart
swell·ing
swept
swerve

swift
swim
swim·ming
swim·suit
swin·dle

swin·dler
swing
swing·ing
switch
switch·board

switched
switches
switch·ing
swivel
swol·len

sworn
swung
syl·labic
syl·la·ble
syl·la·bus

sym·bi·otic
sym·bol
sym·bolic
sym·bol·ism
sym·bol·ize

sym·met·ri·cal
sym·pa·thetic
sym·pa·thize
sym·pa·thy
sym·phonic

sym·phony
sym·po·sia
sym·po·sium
symp·tom
symp·tom·atic

syna·gogue
syn·chro·nize
syn·chro·nous
syn·chro·nously
syn·di·cate

syn·di·cated
syn·di·ca·tion
syn·drome
syn·er·gism
syn·er·gis·tic

syn·fuels
syn·onym
syn·ony·mous
syn·op·sis
syn·tax

syn·the·sis
syn·the·size
syn·the·siz·ing
syn·thetic
sy·ringe

sy·ringes
syrup
sys·tem
sys·tem·atic
sys·tem·ati·cally

sys·tem·atize

_ T _____

tab
tab·er·na·cle
table
tab·leau
ta·bled

ta·bles
table·spoon
tab·let
table·ware
tab·loid

taboo
tabu-lar
tabu-late
tabu-lated
tabu-lat•ing

tabu-la-tion
tabu-la•tor
ta•chome-ter
tacit
taci-turn

tacked
tack-ing
tackle
tack-led
tack-ling

tact
tact-ful
tac-ti•cal
tac-tics
tac-tile

tact-less
taf-feta
tag
tag-board
tagged

tag-ging
tail-ing
tai•lor
tai-lored
tai-lor•ing

take
take-down *(n.)*
taken
take-off *(n.)*
take-over *(n.)*

taker
tak•ers
take--up *(n.)*
tak•ing
tal•ent

tal-ented
tal-is•man
talk
talked
talk-ing

tall
tal-lied
tally
tal-ly•ing
ta•male

tam-bou-rine
tam•per
tam-pered
tan•dem
tan-gent

tan-ger•ine
tan-gi•ble
tan•gle
tan-gled
tank

tank-age
tanker
tan-ning
tan-ta-lize
tan-ta-mount

tan-trum
tap
tape
taped
ta•pered

ta•per-ing
tap-es•try
tap•ing
tapped
tap-ping

tar-dies
tar-di-ness
tardy
tar•get
tar-geted

tar-get•ing
tar•iff
tar-nish
tar-pau•lin
tarry

task
taste
tasted
taste-ful
taste-fully

taste-less
tast-ing
tasty
tat-tered
tat•tle

tat-tling
tat•too
taught
tav•ern
tax

tax-abil•ity
tax-able
taxa-tion
taxed
taxes

taxi
taxi-cab
tax•ied
taxi-der-mist
tax•ing

tax-on•omy
tax-payer
tax-paying
tea
teach

teach-able
teacher
teach-ers
teaches
teach-ing

T

team
teamed
team-ster
team-work
tea·pot

tear
tear-ing
tear-sheet
tease
teased

tea-spoon
tea-spoon-fuls
tech-nic
tech-ni·cal
tech-ni-cali-ties

tech-ni-cal·ity
tech-ni-cally
tech-ni-cian
tech-nique
tech-no-log-ical

tech-nolo-gies
tech-nolo-gist
tech-nol·ogy
te·dious
te·diously

te·dium
teen-age
teen-ager
teeth
tee-to-taler

tele-cast
tele-com-mu-ni-ca-tions
tele-con-fer-enc·ing
tele-fax
tele-gram

tele-graph
te·leg-ra-pher
tele-lec-ture
te·lepa-thy
tele-phone

tele-phoned
tele-phonic
tele-play
tele-printer
tele-scope

tele-scop·ing
tele-thon
tele-type
tele-vise
tele-vi-sion

tell
teller
tell-ers
tell-ing
tel-lu-rium

tem·per
tem-pera-ment
tem-pera-men·tal
tem-per-ance
tem-per·ate

tem-pera-ture
tem-pered
tem-pest
tem-plate
tem·ple

tempo
tem-po·ral
tem-po-rar·ies
tem-po-rar·ily
tem-po-rary

tempt
temp-ta-tion
tempt-ing
ten
ten-able

te·na-cious
te·na-ciously
te·nac-ity
ten-an-cies
ten-ancy

ten·ant
tend
tended
ten-den-cies
ten-dency

ten·der
ten-dered
ten-der·ing
ten-der·ize
ten-der-loin

ten-der-ness
tend-ing
ten·don
tene-ment
Ten-nes·see

ten·nis
tenor
tense
ten-sile
ten-sion

tent
ten-ta·cle
ten-ta-tive
ten-ta-tively
tenth

ten·ure
ten-ured
term
termed
ter-mi·nal

ter-mi-nate
ter-mi-nated
ter-mi-nat·ing
ter-mi-na-tion
ter-mi-nol·ogy

ter-mite
ter-race
ter-rain
ter-rar·ium
ter-razzo

ter-res-trial
ter-ri•ble
ter-ri•bly
ter-rific
ter-ri-fied

ter-rify
ter-ri-to-rial
ter-ri-to-ries
ter-ri-tory
ter•ror

ter-ror•ism
ter-ror•ist
ter-ror•ize
ter-tiary
test

tes-ta-ment
tes-ta-men-tary
tes-tate
tes-ta•tor
tested

tester
tes-ticu•lar
tes-ti-fied
tes-tify
tes-ti-fy•ing

tes-ti-mo-nial
tes-ti-mo-nies
tes-ti-mony
test-ing
Texas

text
text-book
tex-tile
tex-tual
tex-tu-ally

tex-ture
tex-tured
tex-tur•ing
than
thank

thanked
thank-ful
thank-ing
thank-less
thanks-giv•ing

that
thaw
thaw-ing
the
the-ater

the-at-ri•cal
the-at-rics
thee
theft
their

them
theme
them-selves
then
thence-forth

theo-lo-gian
theo-log-ical
the-ol•ogy
theo-rem
theo-ret-ical

theo-reti-cally
theo-ries
theo-rize
the•ory
thera-peu•tic

thera-pist
ther-apy
there
there-abouts
there-after

thereat
thereby
there-fore
there-from
therein

thereof
thereon
thereto
there-to-fore
there-upon

there-with
ther-mal
ther-mally
ther-mo-dy-nam•ics
ther-mo-fluid

ther-mo-stat
the-sau•rus
these
the•ses
the•sis

they
they'll
they're
they've
thick

thicken
thick-en•ing
thicker
thick-ness
thick-nesses

thief
thiev-ery
thieves
thin
thing

think
thinker
think-ers
think-ing
thin-ner

thin-ness
thin-ning
third
thirdly
thirsty

thir-teen
thir-ties
thir-ti•eth
thirty
this

this-tle
thor-ough
thorough-bred
thorough-fare
thor-oughly

those
though
thought
thought-ful
thought-fully

thought-ful-ness
thou-sand
thou-sandth
thrash
thrash-ing

thread
thread-bare
threaded
thread-ing
threat

threaten
threat-ened
threat-en•ing
three
three--fourths

three--quarters
three-some
thresh-old
threw
thrift

thrifty
thrill
thrilled
thrill-ing
thrive

thriv-ing
throat
throb
throb-bing
throt-tle

throt-tling
through
through-out
throw
throw-ing

thrown
thrust
thrust-ing
thumb
thumb-print

thun-der
thun-der•ing
thun-der•ous
thunder-storm
Thurs-day

thus
thy-roid
tick
ticket
tick-eted

tick-et•ing
tick-ets
tickle
tick-ler
tick-lish

tidal
tide-water
tie
tied
tie--in (n.)

tier
tie--up (n.)
tiger
tight
tighten

tight-en•ing
tighter
tightly
tile
tiled

til•ing
till
tilt
tilt-ing
tim•ber

tim-bered
time
timed
time-keeper
time-li-ness

timely
timer
tim•ers
time-saver
time-saving

time-table
time-wise
timid
ti•mid-ity
tim-idly

tim•ing
tin•der
tin-foil
tin•gle
tin•ker

tin•kle
tin•sel
tinted
tiny
tip

tip--off (n.)
tipped
ti•rade
tire
tired

tired-ness
tire-less
tire-lessly
tire-some
tir·ing

tis·sue
ti·tanic
tithe
title
ti·tled

title-holder
ti·tles
ti·tlist
to
toast

toasted
toaster
toast-ing
to·bacco
to·bog-gan

today
tod-dler
to·gether
to·gether-ness
tog·gle

toil
toi·let
token
told
tol-er-able

tol-er-ance
tol-er-ances
tol-er·ant
tol-er·ate
tol-er-ated

tol-er-at·ing
tol·era-tion
toll
toll-booth
toll-gate

to·mato
to·ma-toes
tomb-stone
to·mor-row
ton

tonal
tone
tongue
tonic
to·night

ton-nage
ton·sil
ton-sil-lec-tomy
ton-sil-li·tis
too

took
tool
tooled
tool-ing
tool-maker

tooth
tooth-ache
tooth-brush
tooth-paste
top

top-coat
topic
top-ical
top·ics
top--notch

to·po-graphic
to·po-graph-ical
to·po-graphi-cally
to·pog-ra·phy
topped

top-ping
top-soil
topsy--turvy
torch
tor-ment

torn
tor-nado
tor-na-does
tor-pedo
torque

tor-rent
tor-ren-tial
tor·rid
torso
tort

tor-toise
tor-tu·ous
tor-ture
tor-tur·ous
toss

tossed
tosses
total
to·taled
to·tal-ing

to·tal-ity
touch
touch-down
touched
touches

touch-ing
tough
toughen
tougher
tough-ness

tou·pee
tour
toured
tour-ing
tour-ism

tour-ist
tour-na-ment
tour-ney
tour-ni-quet
touted

to·ward
towed
towel
tow·els
tower

tow-er·ing
tow·ers
tow·ing
town
town house

town houses
town-ship
tox-emia
toxic
tox-ici-ties

tox-ic·ity
toxi-co-log-ical
toxi-col·ogy
toxin
toy

trace
trace-abil·ity
traced
tracer
tra-chea

trac-ing
track
track-age
track-ing
tract

trac-ta·ble
trac-tion
trac-tor
trade
traded

trade--in *(n.)*
trade-mark
trader
trad-ing
tra-di-tion

tra-di-tional
tra-di-tion-ally
traf-fic
trage-dies
trag-edy

tragic
trail
trailed
trailer
trail-ers

trail-ing
train
train-able
trained
trainee

train-ees
trainer
train-ing
traipse
trait

trai-tor
tra-jec-to-ries
tra-jec-tory
tramp
tramp-ing

tram-ple
tram-po-line
tram-way
tran-quil
tran-quil·ize

tran-quil-izer
tran-quil-lity
trans-act
trans-acted
trans-act·ing

trans-ac-tion
trans-at-lan·tic
tran-scend
tran-scen-dent
trans-con-ti-nen·tal

tran-scribe
tran-scribed
tran-scriber
tran-scrib·ers
tran-scrib·ing

tran-script
tran-scrip-tion
trans-fer
trans-fer-able
trans-fer-ence

trans-ferred
trans-fer-ring
trans-form
trans-for-ma-tion
trans-formed

trans-former
trans-fuse
trans-fu-sion
trans-gress
tran-sient

tran-sis·tor
tran-sis-tor·ize
tran-sit
tran-si-tion
tran-si-tional

tran-si-tory
trans-late
trans-lated
trans-lat·ing
trans-la-tion

trans-la·tor
trans-lu-cency
trans-lu-cent
trans-mis-sion
trans-mit

trans-mit·tal
trans-mit·ted
trans-mit·ter
trans-mit-ting
trans-pa-cific

trans-par-en-cies
trans-par-ency
trans-par•ent
tran-spire
tran-spired

trans-plant
trans-port
trans-port-able
trans-por-ta-tion
trans-ported

trans-port•ing
trans-pose
trans-posed
trans-po-si-tion
trans-verse

trans-versely
trap
tra-peze
trapped
trap-per

trap-ping
trash
trauma
trau-matic
tra-vail

travel
trav-eled
trav-eler
trav-el•ers
trav-el•ing

trav-el-ogue
trav-els
tra-verse
trav-esty
trawl-ers

tray
treach-er•ous
treach-ery
trea-son
trea-sure

trea-sured
trea-surer
trea-sur•ers
trea-sury
treat

treated
trea-ties
treat-ing
trea-tise
treat-ment

treaty
tree
trek
trem-ble
trem-bling

tre-men-dous
tre-men-dously
tremor
trench
tren-chant

trench-ing
trend
trend-ing
trepi-da-tion
tres-pass

tres-passes
tres-pass•ing
tress
tres-tle
trial

tri•als
tri-an•gle
tri-an-gu•lar
tribal
tribe

tribu-la-tion
tri-bu•nal
tri-bune
tribu-tar•ies
tribu-tary

trib-ute
trick
trick-ery
trickle
tried

tries
tri•fle
tri-fled
tri-fo•cal
trig-ger

trig-gered
trigo-nome•try
tril-lion
tril-ogy
trim

trimmed
trim-mer
trim-ming
trio
trip

tri-par-tite
tri•ple
tri-pled
trip-let
trip-li-cate

trip-ling
tripped
trip-ping
tri-umph
tri-um-phant

tri-umph•ing
trivia
triv-ial
trol-ley
trom-bone

trooper
troop-ers
tro-phies
tro•phy
tro•pic

trop-ical
trou-ble
trou-bled
trouble-maker
trouble-shooter

trouble-shooting
trou-ble-some
trou-bling
troupe
trou-sers

trowel
tru-ancy
tru-ant
truck
trucker

truck-ers
truck-ing
truck-load
true
tru-ism

truly
trum-pet
trun-cate
trunk
truss

trusses
trust
trustee
trust-ees
trust-ful

trust-ing
trust-worthy
trusty
truth
truth-ful

truth-fully
try
try-ing
try-out
T--shirt

tub
tube
tube-less
tu-ber-cu-lar
tu-ber-cu-lin

tu-ber-cu-lo-sis
tub-ing
tu-bu-lar
tucked
Tues-day

tu-ition
tulip
tum-ble
tum-bled
tum-bler

tum-bling
tumor
tu-mul-tu-ous
tuna
tune

tuner
tune--up *(n.)*
tung-sten
tun-ing
tun-nel

tur-bine
tur-bo-charged
tur-bo-charger
tur-bo-jet
tur-bo-prop

tur-bu-lence
tur-bu-lent
tur-key
tur-moil
turn

turn-about
turn-around
turn-down *(n.)*
turned
turn-ing

turn-key
turn-out
turn-over
turn-pike
turn-table

tur-pen-tine
tur-quoise
tu-te-lage
tutor
tu-tored

tu-tor-ing
tux-edo
tweed
twelfth
twelve

twen-ties
twen-ti-eth
twenty
twice
twi-light

twin
twin-kle
twin-kling
twist
twisted

twist-ing
two
two-fold
two--thirds
ty-coon

tying
type
typed
type-setting
type-write

type-writer
type-writers
type-writing
type-written
typ-ical

typi-cally
typ•ify
typ•ing
typ•ist
typo

ty•po-graph-ical
ty•ran-ni•cal
tyr-anny
ty•rant

_U

ubiq-ui-tous
ubiq-uity
ugly
uku-lele
ulcer

ul•te-rior
ul•ti-mate
ul•ti-mately
ul•ti-ma•tum
ul•tra-mod•ern

ul•tra-sonic
ul•tra-sound
um•bil-ical
um•brella
um•pire

un•abashed
un•able
un•abridged
un•ac-cept-able
un•ac-count-able

un•ac-counted
un•ac-cred-ited
un•ac-cus-tomed
un•af-fected
un•afraid

un•aided
un•al-ter-able
una-nim•ity
unani-mous
unani-mously

un•an-nounced
un•an-swer-able
un•an-swered
un•an-tici-pated
un•ap-proach-able

un•ap-pro-pri-ated
un•ap-proved
un•armed
un•as-signed
un•as-sum•ing

un•at-tached
un•at-tain-able
un•at-tended
un•at-trac-tive
un•au-tho-rized

un•avail-abil•ity
un•avail-able
un•avoid-able
un•avoid-ably
un•aware

un•bal-anced
un•bear-able
un•beat-able
un•be-com•ing
un•be-liev-able

un•be-liev-ably
un•bend-ing
un•bi-ased
un•break-able
un•bro-ken

un•canny
un•cer-tain
un•cer-tain-ties
un•cer-tainty
un•changed

un•civi-lized
un•claimed
un•clas-si-fi-able
un•clas-si-fied
uncle

un•clean
un•clut-tered
un•col-lected
un•col-lect-ible
un•com-fort-able

un•com-mit•ted
un•com-mon
un•com-pleted
un•com-pli-cated
un•com-pro-mis•ing

un•con-cerned
un•con-di-tional
un•con-di-tion-ally
un•con-scious
un•con-sti-tu-tional

un•con-trol-la•ble
un•con-trolled
un•con-ven-tional
un•co-op-era-tive
un•co-or-di-nated

un•cover
uncut
un•de-cided
un•de-fined
un•de-liv-er-able

un•de-liv-ered
un•de-ni-able
un•de-pend-able
under
un•der-achiever

un•der-age
un•der-charge
un•der-cover
un•der-cut
un•der-de-vel-oped

un•der-dog
un•der-em-ploy-ment
un•der-foot
un•dergo
un•der-go•ing

un•der-gone
un•der-gradu•ate
un•der-ground
un•der-hand
un•der-handed

un•der-lie
un•der-line
un•der-lined
un•der-lin•ing
un•der-ly•ing

un•der-mine
un•der-neath
un•der-paid
un•der-pass
un•der-pay-ment

un•der-priced
un•der-privi-leged
un•der-score
un•der-scor•ing
un•der-signed

un•der-sized
un•der-staffed
un•der-stand
un•der-stand-able
un•der-stand-ably

un•der-stand•ing
un•der-stated
un•der-state-ment
un•der-stood
un•der-study

un•der-take
un•der-taken
un•der-taker
un•der-tak•ing
un•der-took

un•der-used
un•der-uti-lize
un•der-wa•ter
un•der-way *(adj.)*
under way *(adv.)*

un•der-write
un•der-writer
un•der-writ•ing
un•der-writ•ten
un•de-sir-able

un•de-tected
un•de-ter-mined
un•de-vel-op-able
un•de-vel-oped
un•dig-ni-fied

un•dis-ci-plined
un•dis-closed
un•dis-puted
un•dis-turbed
un•di-vided

undo
un•do-ing
un•done
un•doubt-edly
undue

un•duly
un•dy-ing
un•earned
un•earthly
un•easi-ness

un•easy
un•eco-nom-ical
un•edu-cated
un•em-ploy-able
un•em-ployed

un•em-ploy-ment
un•en-force-able
un•en-forced
un•equal
un•equaled

un•equipped
un•equivo-cal
un•equivo-cally
un•eth-ical
un•even

un•event-ful
un•ex-cused
un•ex-pected
un•ex-pect-edly
un•ex-pended

un•ex-plained
un•fail-ing
un•fair
un•fairly
un•faith-ful

un•fa-mil•iar
un•fa-vor-able
un•fa-vor-ably
un•fea-si•ble
un•filled

un•fin-ished
unfit
un•fold
un•fold-ing
un•fore-see-able

un•fore-seen
un•for-get-ta•ble
un•for-tu-nate
un•for-tu-nately
un•founded

un•friendly
un•fruit-ful
un•fur-nished
un•godly
un•grate-ful

un•guarded
un•hal-lowed
un•hap-pily
un•hap-pi-ness
un•happy

un·healthy
un·heard
un·hesi-tat·ing
un·hur-ried
un·iden-ti-fied

uni-fi-ca-tion
uni-fied
uni-fies
uni-form
uni-for-mity

uni-formly
unify
uni-lat-eral
uni-lat-er-ally
un·imag-in-able

un·im-peach-able
un·im-por-tant
un·im-proved
un·in-cor-po-rated
un·in-formed

un·in-spired
un·in-sur-able
un·in-sured
un·in-tel-li-gi·ble
un·in-tended

un·in-ten-tional
un·in-ter-ested
un·in-ter-est·ing
un·in-ter-rupted
union

union-ize
unique
uniquely
unique-ness
uni·son

unit
unite
united
unit-ing
unit-ize

unity
uni-ver·sal
uni-ver-sally
uni-verse
uni-ver-si-ties

uni-ver-sity
un·just
un·jus-ti-fi-able
un·jus-ti-fi-ably
un·kempt

un·kind
un·know-ing
un·known
un·law-ful
un·law-fully

un·leaded
un·less
un·like
un·like-li-hood
un·likely

un·lim-ited
un·listed
un·load
un·loaded
un·load-ing

un·lock
un·locked
un·lucky
un·man-age-able
un·mar-ket-able

un·mar-ried
un·matched
un·men-tion-able
un·mis-tak-able
un·natu-ral

un·natu-rally
un·nec-es-sar·ily
un·nec-es-sary
un·needed
un·no-ticed

un·num-bered
un·ob-tain-able
un·oc-cu-pied
un·of-fi-cially
un·opened

un·op-posed
un·or-ga-nized
un·pack
un·pack-ing
un·paid

un·par-al-leled
un·par-don-able
un·planned
un·pleas-ant
un·prece-dented

un·pre-dict-able
un·pre-pared
un·pre-ten-tious
un·pro-duc-tive
un·pro-fes-sional

un·prof-it-able
un·pro-tected
un·proven
un·quali-fied
un·ques-tion-able

un·ques-tion-ably
un·ques-tioned
un·read-able
un·re-al-is·tic
un·re-al-ized

un·rea-son-able
un·rea-son-ably
un·re-corded
un·re-lated
un·re-li-abil·ity

un·re-li-able
un·re-ported
un·re-solved
un·re-spon-sive
un·rest

un•re-strained
un•re-stricted
un•righ-teous
un•roll
un•ruly

un•safe
un•sal-able
un•sani-tary
un•sat-is-fac-tory
un•sat-is-fied

un•satu-rated
un•sa-vory
un•scru-pu-lous
un•sea-son-ably
un•se-cured

un•seemly
un•seen
un•self-ish
un•self-ishly
un•set-tled

un•sightly
un•signed
un•skilled
un•so-cia•ble
un•sold

un•so-lic-ited
un•so-phis-ti-cated
un•speak-able
un•spon-sored
un•struc-tured

un•suc-cess•ful
un•suc-cess-fully
un•suit-able
un•su-per-vised
un•sup-ported

un•sure
un•sur-passed
un•tan-gle
un•tapped
un•ten-able

un•thank-ful
un•think-able
until
un•timely
un•tir-ing

unto
un•told
un•touch-able
un•touched
un•trained

un•tried
un•trim
un•truth-ful
un•us-able
un•used

un•usual
un•usu-ally
un•wanted
un•war-ranted
un•wel-come

un•will-ing
un•will-ing-ness
un•wise
un•wit-tingly
un•work-able

un•wor-thy
un•wrap
un•writ-ten
up
up•beat

up•bring-ing
up•com-ing
up•date
up•dated
up•dat-ing

up•grade
up•graded
up•grad-ing
up•heaval
up•held

up•hold
up•hold-ing
up•hol-stered
up•hol-stery
up•keep

up•lift-ing
upon
upper
up•per-most
up•right

up•ris-ing
up•roar
up•root
upset
up•set-ting

up•side
up•stairs
up•state
up•stream
up•surge

up•tight
up•town
up•turn
up•ward
ura-nium

urban
ur•ban-ized
urge
urged
ur•gency

ur•gent
ur•gently
urges
urg•ing
uri•nal

uri-naly•sis
uri-nary
uro-log-ical
urolo-gist
urol-ogy

us
us•abil•ity
us•able
usage
use

used
use•ful
use-fully
use-ful-ness
use-less

user
uses
usher
using
usual

usu-ally
usurp
usury
Utah
uten-sil

utili-tar•ian
utili-ties
util-ity
uti-li-za-tion
uti-lize

uti-lized
uti-lizes
uti-liz•ing
ut•most
ut•ter-ance

ut•ter-ances
ut•ter-ing

V _____

va•can-cies
va•cancy
va•cant
va•cate
va-cated

va•cat-ing
va•ca-tion
va•ca-tion•ing
vac-ci-nate
vac-ci-na-tion

vac-cine
vac-il-late
vac-uum
vaga-bond
va•grancy

va•grant
vague
vaguely
vain
vale-dic-to-rian

vale-dic-tory
val-en-tine
valet
val-iant
valid

vali-date
vali-dated
vali-da-tion
va•lidi-ties
va•lid-ity

val•ley
valor
valu-able
valu-ation
value

val•ued
valve
valv-ing
van
van•dal

van-dal•ism
van-dal-ized
va•nilla
van•ish
van-ishes

van-ish•ing
van•ity
van-tage
vapor
va•por-iz•ing

vari-abil•ity
vari-able
vari-ance
vari-ances
varia-tion

vari-cose
var•ied
var•ies
va•ri-et•ies
va•ri-ety

vari-ous
vari-ously
var-nish
var-nishes
var-sity

vary
vary-ing
vas-cu•lar
vase
Vase-line

vast
vastly
vaude-ville
vault
vaulted

veered
vege-ta•ble
vege-tar•ian
vege-tate
vege-ta-tion

ve•he-mence
ve•he-ment
ve•hi-cle
ve•hicu-lar
vein

ve•loc-ity
ve•lour
vel•vet
vel•vety
vendee

vend-ing
ven•dor
ve•neer
ven-er-able
ve•ne-real

ven-geance
venge-ful
ven-om•ous
vent
vented

ven-ti-late
ven-ti-lat•ing
ven-ti-la-tion
ven-ti-la•tor
ven-ti-la-tory

vent-ing
ven-trilo-quism
ven-trilo-quist
ven-ture
ven-tured

ven-ture-some
ven-tur•ous
ve•ra-cious
ve•rac-ity
ver•bal

ver-bal•ize
ver-bal-ized
ver-bally
ver-ba•tim
ver-biage

ver-bose
ver-dict
veri-fi-ca-tion
veri-fied
veri-fier

veri-fies
ver-ify
veri-fy•ing
ver•ily
veri-ta•ble

Ver-mont
ver-nacu•lar
ver-sa-tile
ver-sa-til•ity
verse

versed
verses
ver-sion
ver•sus
ver-te•bra

ver-te-brae
ver-ti•cal
ver-ti-cally
ver-tigo
very

ves•per
ves•sel
vest
vested
ves-ti-bule

vest-ing
vest-ment
ves•try
vet-eran
vet-er•ans

vet-eri-nar•ian
vet-eri-nary
veto
ve•toed
vexa-tion

vex•ing
via
via-bil•ity
vi•able
via-duct

vibes
vi•brant
vi•brate
vi•brat-ing
vi•bra-tion

vi•bra-tor
vi•bra-tory
vi•cari-ous
vi•cari-ously
vice--president

vice--principal
vices
vice versa
vi•cini-ties
vi•cin-ity

vi•cious
vi•cis-si-tude
vic•tim
vic-tim•ize
vic•tor

vic-to-ri•ous
vic-tory
vict-ual
video
vid-eo-tape

vid-eo-taped
view
view-able
viewed
viewer

view-graph
view-ing
view-point
vigil
vigi-lance

vigi-lant
vigor
vig-or•ous
vig-or-ously
vil•ify

villa
vil-lage
vil-lain
vil-lain•ous
vin-ci•ble

vin-di-cate
vin-di-ca-tion
vin-dic-tive
vine-gar
vine-yard

vin-tage
vinyl
vi•nyls
vio-late
vio-lated

vio-lat•ing
vio-la-tion
vio-la•tor
vio-lence
vio-lent

vio-lently
vio•let
vio•lin
vir•gin
Vir-ginia

vir•ile
vir-tual
vir-tu-ally
vir•tue
vir-tu•oso

vir-tu•ous
virus
visa
vis--à--vis
vis-cos•ity

visi-bil•ity
vis-ible
vi•sion
visit
visi-ta-tion

vis-ited
vis-it•ing
visi-tor
vis•its
visor

vista
vi•sual
vi•su-al-iza-tion
vi•su-al•ize
vi•su-ally

vital
vi•tal-ity
vi•tal-iz•ing
vi•tally
vi•ta-min

vi•ti-ate
vit-re•ous
vit-ri-olic
vi•va-cious
vi•vac-ity

vivid
viv-idly
vo•cabu-lary
vocal
vo•cal-ist

vo•cal-ize
vo•ca-tion
vo•ca-tional
vo•ca-tion-ally
vo•cif-er•ous

voice
voiced
voices
void
void-ing

vola-tile
vol-cano
vo•li-tion
vol•ley
volley-ball

volt
volt-age
volt-ages
vol•ume
volu-met•ric

vo•lu-mi-nous
vol-un-tarily
vol-un-tary
vol-un-teer
vol-un-teered

vol-un-teer•ing
vo•ra-cious
vote
voter
vot•ers

vot•ing
vouch
vouched
voucher
vouch-ers

vouch-safe
vowel
voy•age
vul•gar
vul-nera-bil•ity

vul-ner-able
vul-ture
vying

___ W _____

wafer
wa•fers
waf•fle
wage
waged

wager
wages
wagon
waist
wait

waited
waiter
wait-ing
wait-ress
wait-resses

waive
waived
waiver
waiv-ers
waiv-ing

wake
wak•ing
walk
walka-thon
walked

walker
walk-ing
walk--on *(n.)*
walk-out *(n.)*
walk-way

wall
wall-board
wal•let
wall-paper
wal•nut

wan•der
wan-derer
wan-der•ing
want
wanted

want-ing
wan•ton
war
ward
war•den

ward-robe
ware-house
ware-housed
ware-houses
ware-housing

war-fare
war-head
warily
warm
warmed

warm-est
warm-ing
warmly
warmth
warm--up *(n.)*

warn
warned
warn-ing
warp
warp-ing

war-rant
war-ranted
war-ran-ties
war-rant•ing
war-ranty

war-rior
war-ship
war-time
wary
was

wash
wash-able
washed
washer
wash-ers

wash-ing
Wash-ing•ton
wash-room
wasn't
waste

waste-basket
waste-ful
waste-land
waste-paper
waste-water

wast-ing
watch
watch-dog
watched
watches

watch-ful
watch-ing
watch-maker
water
water-borne

water-color
water-craft
wa•tered
water-flood
water-flow

water-fowl
water-front
wa•ter-ing
water-mark
water-melon

water-proof
water-proofing
wa•ters
water-shed
water-way

water-works
wa•tery
watt
watt-age
wave

waver
wav•ing
wax
wax•ing
waxy

way
way-bill
way-faring
way•lay
way-side

way-ward
we
weak
weaken
weak-ened

weak-en·ing
weak-ens
weaker
weak-est
weak-ness

weak-nesses
wealth
wealthy
weapon
weap-ons

wear
wear-ing
wea-ri-some
weary
weather

weath-ered
weath-er·ing
weath-er-iz·ing
weave
weaver

weav-ing
web
web-bing
wed
wed-ding

wed-lock
Wednes·day
weed
week
week-day

week-end
week-lies
weekly
weep
weep-ing

wee·vil
weigh
weighed
weigh-ing
weight

weighted
weight-ing
weight-less
weight-lifter
weird

wel-come
wel-comed
wel-com·ing
weld
welded

welder
weld-ing
wel-fare
well
well--being

went
were
weren't
west
west-erly

west-ern
west-erner
west-ern·ize
West Vir·ginia
west-ward

wet
wet-land
wet-ness
wet-ting
we've

whale
whal-ing
wharf
wharf-age
what

what-ever
what-so-ever
wheat
wheel
wheel-barrow

wheel-chair
wheeled
wheel-ing
wheeze
wheezes

when
when-ever
where
where-abouts
whereas

whereby
where-fore
wherein
whereof
where-so-ever

whereto
wher-ever
whether
which
which-ever

while
whim
whim-per
whim-si·cal
whip

whip-lash
whipped
whip-ping
whirl-pool
whirl-wind

whis-key
whis-per
whis-tle
whis-tling
white

whit-est
white-wall
white-wash
whither
whit-tle

who
who-ever
whole
whole-hearted
whole-heartedly

whole-sale
whole-saler
whole-salers
whole-saling
whole-some

wholly
whom
whom-ever
whose
why

wicked
wicket
wide
widely
widen

wid-ened
wid-en-ing
wider
wide-spread
wid-est

widow
wid-ower
width
width-wise
wie-ner

wife
wig-gle
wild
wild-cat
wil-der-ness

wild-est
wild-life
will
will-ful
will-fully

will-ing
will-ingly
will-ing-ness
wil-low
will-power

win
wind
winded
wind-fall
wind-ing

wind-mill
win-dow
wind-screen
wind-shield
wind-storm

wind-ward
wine
win-ery
wing
win-kle

win-ner
win-ning
win-ter
win-ter-ize
winter-time

win-try
wipe
wiper
wire
wire-cutter

wired
wire-less
wire-tapping
wir-ing
Wis-con-sin

wis-dom
wise
wisely
wiser
wish

wished
wishes
wish-ful
wish-ing
wist-ful

with
with-draw
with-draw-able
with-drawal
with-draw-als

with-draw-ing
with-drawn
with-drew
wither
with-held

with-hold
with-hold-ing
within
with-out
with-stand

with-stand-ing
with-stood
wit-ness
wit-nessed
wit-nesses

wit-ness-ing
witty
wives
wiz-ard
wob-ble

woe-ful
woe-fully
woman
women
won

won·der
won-dered
won-der·ful
won-der-ful·ly
won-der·ing

won-der-land
won-ders
won-drous
won't
wood

wooded
wooden
wood-land
wood-pecker
wood-work

wood-working
woody
wool
woolen
word

worded
word-ing
wore
work
work-abil·ity

work-able
work-book
work-day
worked
worker

work-ers
work force
work-ing
work load
work-out *(n.)*

work-place
work-room
work-sharing
work-sheet
work-shop

work-week
world
worldly
world-wide
worn

wor-ried
wor-ries
wor-ri-some
worry
wor-ry·ing

worse
worsen
wors-en·ing
wor-ship
wor-shiped

worst
wor-sted
worth
wor-thier
wor-thi-ness

worth-less
worth-while
wor·thy
would
wouldn't

wound
wounded
woven
wran-gle
wran-gler

wrap
wrapped
wrap-per
wrap-ping
wrath-ful

wreath
wreck
wreck-age
wrecked
wrecker

wrench
wrenches
wres-tle
wres-tling
wretched

wringer
wrin-kle
wrist-watch
write
write--in *(n.)*

write--off *(n.)*
writer
writ-ers
write--up *(n.)*
writ-ing

writ-ten
wrong
wrong-doing
wrong-ful
wrongly

wrote
wrought
Wyo-ming

_X_

xe·rog-ra·phy
xerox *(v.)*
xe·roxed
xe·rox-ing
X ray *(n.)*

x--ray *(v.)*
xy·lo-phone

_Y_

yacht
yacht-ing
yard
yard-age
yard-stick

yarn
yawn
year
year-book
year--end

yearly
yearn-ing
yell-ing
yel•low
yes

yes-ter•day
yes-ter-year
yet
yield
yielded

yield-ing
yo•gurt
yoke
yolk
yon•der

you
you'd
you'll
young
youn-ger

youn-gest
young-ster
your
you're
your-self

your-selves
youth
youth-ful
you've
yule-tide

_Z_____

zagged
zag-ging
zeal
zealot
zeal-ous

zebra
ze•nith
zero
ze•roed
zest

zest-ful
zig•zag
zinc
zip
zip code

zipped
zip•per
zo•diac
zom•bie
zonal

zone
zoned
zon•ing
zoo-log-ical
zo•olo-gist

zo•ol-ogy
zoom
zoom-ing
zuc-chini